Mother Goose in Stitches

Kathleen Thorne-Thomsen

Holt, Rinehart and Winston
New York

For Linda, Germaine,
and the Magic Red Bear

Published simultaneously in Canada by Holt, Rinehart
and Winston of Canada, Limited.

Library of Congress Cataloging in Publication Data

Thorne-Thomsen, Kathleen.
Mother Goose in stitches.

1. Embroidery—Patterns. I. Title.
TT771.T43   746.4'4   75-21486
ISBN 0-03-015201-1

First Edition

Designer: Kathleen Thorne-Thomsen
Printed in the United States of America

10 9 8 7 6 5 4 3 2 1

Acknowledgments

There are several wonderful people whose assistance in this project must be acknowledged, for without them I would most certainly have missed a couple of stitches along the way. No matter what I say here, it will not be adequate. I can only try to thank them.

A very special place in my heart is reserved for Linda Brownridge, who rendered all the line illustrations and many of the patterns. Her extraordinary kindness and understanding during the many days spent on the project provided me with moral support, while her expert knowledge of design and creative use of fashions and needlework materially contributed to the book.

I also want to express my thanks to Tom Brosterman for shooting the black and white photographs. As my partner in a graphic-design office during the book's production, he provided creative input at every step. Tom was also responsible for the concept behind many of the patterns. My thanks to Robert Bassett for his fine color photography.

I am indebted to my oldest friend Patricia Lewis, and my newest friends Al Halpern and Ronnie Brosterman, for making sense of my notes, and for assisting with the text.

Sincere thanks go to Peri Winkler, my agent, and to Ellyn Polshek, my editor—two superb people who mean much more to me than just business associates.

For taking the time to stitch up and test my patterns, I am most grateful to Ruth Bucholz and to my mother, Viola McDonald; also to my friends Mimi Malenius Jasinski and Pam Erenberg; and to my cousin Eileen Zadrow.

Storekeepers Albert and Ilse Wiener, Richard Barili, William Doyne, and Linda Ashton were most helpful with research, and I am indebted to them.

A vote of thanks is due Jess DeAnda, of DeAnda Lithograph, Los Angeles, and Fred Schindler, of Headliners, Los Angeles, for their help with reproducing illustrations.

And, finally, I am grateful to Mary Thorne-Thomsen who many months ago inspired me to think about doing cross-stitch patterns and compiling them into a book; and to my good friend Richard Perlman for always cheering me up and bolstering my confidence on those dark days when I thought I couldn't possibly meet a deadline.

To all I humbly say "Thank you."

Contents

Description of Color Illustrations 8

Introduction 9

Materials 10
  Yarn 11
  Thread 12
  Cloth 14
  Canvas 16
  Needles 17
  Accessories 17

Stitches 18
  Continental 18
  Basket-weave 19
  Half-cross 20
  Cross 21
  French Knot 22
  Outline 22
  Backstitch 22

Patterns 23
  General Procedures 23

Basic Project 1: 26
  How to Work a Pattern on Aida Cloth
  Little Tommy Tucker 25
  A framed wall piece

Basic Project 2: 28
  How to Work a Pattern on Canvas
  Little Miss Muffet 30
  A pillow

Little Bo-peep 31
Hey diddle, diddle 32/33
There was an old woman
  tossed up in a basket 34
Three wise men of Gotham 35
Humpty Dumpty 36
A red dot of sun comes up 38
Sing a song of sixpence 40
Peter, Peter, pumpkin eater 41
In spring I look gay 42
Great A, little a 44
Higglety, pigglety, pop! 45
Snow, snow faster 46
Molly, my sister and I fell out 48
Jack be nimble 49
Old Mother Goose,
  when she wanted to wander (I) 50
The greedy man is he who sits 51
Ring-a-ring o' roses 52
"No, no, my melodies will never die" 53
Cackle, cackle, Mother Goose 54
To market, to market,
  to buy a fat pig 55
Mother Goose Sampler 56
Old Mother Goose,
  when she wanted to wander (II) 57
Cuckoo, cuckoo, cherry tree 58
A, B, C, and D 60
Jack and Jill 61
March winds and April showers 62
What are little girls made of? 63
Roses are red 64/65
There was a little man 66
Cock-a-doodle-doo! 67
Tom, Tom, the piper's son 68
Old Mother Hubbard 69
There was a fat man of Bombay 70

Needlepoint Applications
Projects, Patterns, and Ideas 71
  Polly put the kettle on 72
  A tea cozy
  Hinx minx 76
  A needlepoint rug
  Hickory, dickory, dock 80
  A clock face
  There was an old woman
    who lived in a shoe 82
  A child's smock
  Goosey, goosey, gander 86
  Old Mother Goose,
    she had a son Jack 88/89
  Mother Goose Family
  A quilt
  Pussy cat, pussy cat 92
  A stuffed toy

Glossary 95

Suppliers 96

Description of Color Illustrations

Plate 1. **Little Tommy Tucker**, a framed wall piece, worked in cross-stitch with cotton embroidery floss on Pearl Aida cloth. Stitched by Pam Erenberg.

Plate 2. **Little Miss Muffet**, a pillow, worked in continental stitch with Persian wool on interlock canvas. Stitched by Ronnie Brosterman.

Plate 3. **Hey diddle, diddle**, two pillows, worked in continental stitch with Persian wool on interlock canvas. Stitched by Mimi Malenius Jasinski.

Plate 4. **Hickory, dickory, dock**, a clock face, worked in cross-stitch with cotton embroidery floss on Pearl Aida cloth. Stitched by Ruth Bucholz. Clock made by John Thorne-Thomsen.

Plate 5. **Polly put the kettle on**, a tea cozy, worked in cross-stitch with cotton embroidery floss on Pearl Aida cloth. Stitched by Viola McDonald.

Plate 6. **Pussy cat, pussy cat**, a stuffed toy, worked in basket-weave stitch with Persian wool on interlock canvas. Stitched by Viola McDonald.

Plate 7. **Hinx minx**, an area rug, worked in basket-weave with Scheepjes rug wool on interlock canvas. Stitched by Kathleen Thorne-Thomsen.

Plate 8. **Cuckoo, cuckoo, cherry tree** (a family tree), a framed wall piece, worked in thread-count cross-stitch with linen floss on an even-weave cotton. Stitched by Ruth Bucholz.

Plate 9. **Mother Goose sampler**, a framed wall piece, worked in cross-stitch with cotton embroidery floss on Pearl Aida cloth. Stitched by Ruth Bucholz.

Plate 10. **Mother Goose Family**, a quilt, worked in cross-stitch with Persian wool over scrim canvas. Quilt sewn by Linda Brownridge; stitched by Ruth Bucholz and Eileen Zadrow.

Plate 11. **There was an old woman who lived in a shoe**, a child's smock, worked in cross-stitch with cotton embroidery floss on Pearl Aida cloth. Dress designed and sewn by Linda Brownridge; stitched by Ruth Bucholz.

Plate 12. **Old Mother Goose**, a framed wall piece, worked in half-cross stitch with Persian wool on interlock canvas. Stitched by Kathleen Thorne-Thomsen.

Introduction

Mother Goose in Stitches is a collection of patterns for needlework inspired by the Mother Goose rhymes familiar to children all over the world since the eighteenth century. This book has been created for everyone who loves Mother Goose—the images conjured up, the rhymes imprinted in our memories. It is for the young and for the young-in-heart who delight in making things. While the book is of special interest to all beginners and intermediates, accomplished needleworkers can use *Mother Goose in Stitches* as a spawning place for ideas and can apply their own advanced techniques and expertise to the patterns. Children will delight in the book as they enter the fantasy world of Mother Goose pictures and rhymes—of performing cats, acrobatic cows and nimble kids. Even youngsters can learn how to do needlework from this book.

The patterns in *Mother Goose in Stitches* are based on English-American samplers of the eighteenth and nineteenth centuries. These samplers, with their balanced and orderly arrangement of colors and stitches, were once used as an instrument of children's education. While practicing to make neat rows of stitches, the children not only learned the alphabet and color coordination, but they created a charming piece of art, albeit primitive by today's standards. The simple way of life represented in these samplers is a way of life which adults find difficult to recap-

ture and often look back upon with a special nostalgia. Because the sampler, as well as the Mother Goose rhyme, belongs to the child, the patterns in *Mother Goose in Stitches* have been created in the traditional children's art form. They will, however, delight everyone, no matter what age, and the finished piece of work will add beauty and gaiety to any room in your house, from the nursery to the living room.

You needn't have any previous experience in needlework to understand and enjoy this book. All that is needed is a fondness for working with your hands and patience, patience, patience. Once you are familiar with stitch techniques and are equipped with the proper materials, you are ready to begin a project. Even a hitherto inexperienced grandfather or father, uncle or nephew can stitch up a magnificent canvas!

For simplicity's sake, only the most basic needlepoint stitches are illustrated in *Mother Goose in Stitches*. These are all you really need to know to accomplish a design, but, of course, an advanced stitcher may embellish a design by using more complex stitches. However, in keeping with the tradition of these patterns, simple stitches will turn out an authentic-looking, beautiful piece of needlework. For further reference, *The New York Times Book of Needlepoint* by Elaine Slater is an excellent dictionary of needlepoint stitches.

Any of these designs may be worked as a rug or a wall hanging on a large mesh canvas using appropriate yarns. The chapter on Needlepoint Applications at the end of the book gives specific information on some special projects that you may wish to undertake. I hope that *Mother Goose in Stitches* will provide you with a fresh new look at these favorite old rhymes and bring you that unique pleasure that comes with creating your own handmade things.

Materials

Paternayan Persian wool

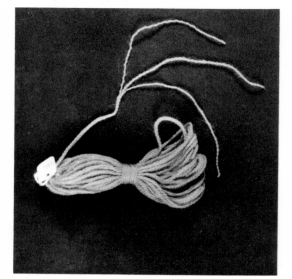

Bucilla Persian wool

DMC tapestry wool

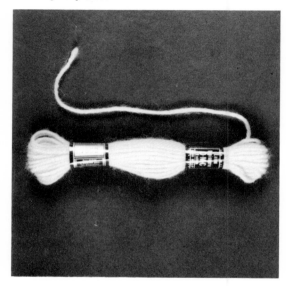

Anchor tapestry wool

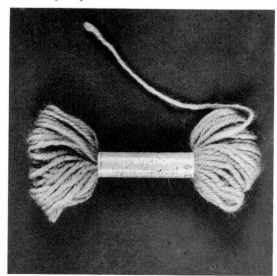

Colbert tapestry wool

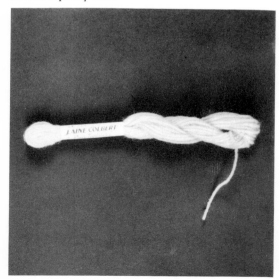

Scheepjes rug wool

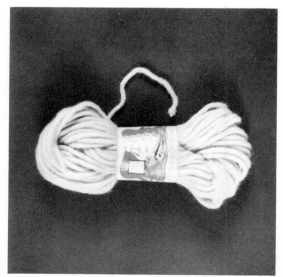

Yarn

Persian Wool: The most common woolen yarn used for needlepoint is Persian wool. It is spun from long-fibered virgin wool which renders it very strong. No other wool is better for durability and for coverage of your canvas.

The Paternayan brand of Persian wool is offered in over 600 colors, but readily available in about 360. It is colorfast, mothproof, and of superb quality. Paternayan (or Paterna) wool may be purchased in 160–200 yard skeins, or in precut lengths (usually 24 inches) by the ounce, or in one continuous length. Most stores will break a skein into smaller amounts for you.

Each length of wool pulled from the hank is composed of three separate strands of 2-ply* wool. These strands may be used in various numbers depending upon the size of your canvas mesh*. To separate one strand from a group of three, hold two of the strands tightly and pull the third away with an upward movement of your arm.

Because of the hairy surface of Persian wool, it is advisable to first work the very dark colors of a pattern before filling in with the lighter shades. Stitching in this order will prevent light colors from being covered with the hairs of the darker wool. Since many brands of woolen yarn are available, you may find others of a similar weight—Bucilla, or Bernat, for example —that will serve your purpose well.

* See glossary on page 95 for definition of term whenever this asterisk appears throughout the book.

Tapestry Wool: Another yarn that is used in needlepoint is DMC (Dollfus-Mieg & Cie) tapestry wool. This yarn is packaged in small 40-yard skeins and is a single strand of 4-ply wool.

Anchor tapestry wool is a thinner type than DMC tapestry wool. It is manufactured by the J.P. Coats Company (the British equivalent of the American Coats & Clark). Packaged in 15-yard skeins, it is one strand of 4-ply wool. Anchor would probably be used on a finer canvas where DMC would be too thick and bulky.

Where a very fine wool is desired, crewel yarn is the best choice. Le Bon Parheur and Colbert (French wools) are considered probably the finest in quality. Some stores carry the completeline of Penelope crewel wools. Also, Paternayan offers a crewel which generally can be special-ordered by stores that carry their Persian wool.

If you plan to do your stitching on clothing, such as a panel to be appliquéd on a Levi jacket, there is a 2-ply/3-strand acrylic by Bernat that may be used without fear of it shrinking.

Rug Yarn: Rug yarns are spun for extra strength. They are thick and durable. These yarns are most often made from three different fibers: wool, Orlon, and acrylic. Acrylic yarn has the tightest twist and is the easiest to work with. Both Orlon and acrylic colors are brighter and have more sheen than wool. However, woolen yarn has the best texture of all. If you choose a good brand, there should be no noticeable difference in the durability of any of these three fibers. Brunswick and Reynolds are two manufacturers whose products are held in high esteem by experts, but Bernat, Spinnerin, Bucilla, and Paternayan also make rug yarns of good quality.

The most beautiful and the most expensive rug yarn is Scheepjes Rya wool, imported from Holland. Scheepjes is a worsted* wool and is available in colors.

Rug yarns are generally available in both skeins and in precut lengths for latch hooking*, with the exception of Scheepjes which usually is available only in skeins.

Six-strand embroidery floss

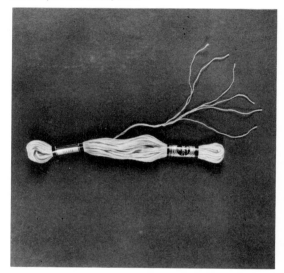

Pearl cotton

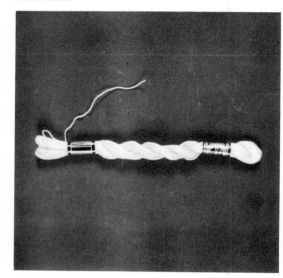

Retors à Broder

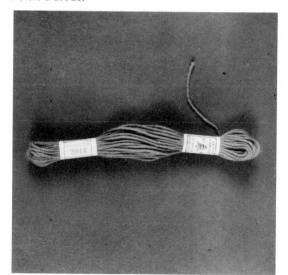

Linen

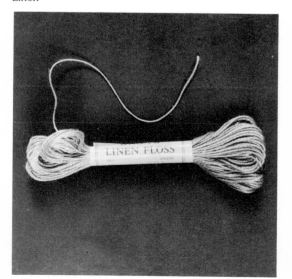

Silk

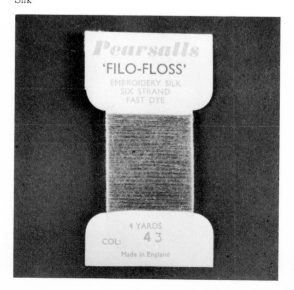

Thread

Six-Strand Embroidery Floss: The most common of cotton threads is 6-strand embroidery floss. It is composed of 6 strands of 2-ply cotton—hence its name. Any number of strands may be used depending upon the size of your stitch and the effect you wish to achieve. Separate the strands in the same manner as previously described for Persian wool.

DMC and Coats and Clark both manufacture 6-strand floss. The DMC floss is most often found in department stores, needlepoint shops, and other specialty wool and yarn stores. It comes in over 300 colors and is packaged in small pull skeins of 8.7 yards each.

Coats and Clark 6-strand floss is sold in variety stores and fabric stores. It is slightly less expensive than the DMC floss, but the choice of colors is more limited. For instance, neither a bright red nor strong yellow may be found in the Coats and Clark selection of floss.

Pearl Cotton: DMC also manufactures Pearl cotton, a slightly different embroidery floss which comes in one 2-ply strand and should not be separated. It has a tight twist and a satinlike sheen which gives the finished stitches a "pearly" look. Although there is a difference in surface texture, Pearl cotton may be used alongside a 6-strand floss for an interesting effect. Pearl cotton comes in four weights: 3, 5, 8, and 12—12 being the thinnest. Again, the color range is a bit more limited than for DMC 6-strand floss. Pearl cotton is sold in both skeins and balls.

A continuous skein of Pearl cotton does not pull apart. To cut a length of this thread, untwist the skein and completely cut through it at one end. Braid the strands together to prevent them from knotting, and pull out one strand at a time as needed.

Retors à Broder: Retors à Broder is a heavy single strand (5-ply) of matte cotton thread which, while being very strong and durable, has a soft texture. It is slightly thicker than the heaviest Pearl cotton (#3) and has a dull, woollike appearance. Use it instead of wool in the case of an allergic reaction or because of shrinkage in laundering. Retors à Broder is manufactured by the DMC company. It is packaged in small pull skeins, and the color range is excellent.

Linen: If you are looking for an unusual effect, linen floss has an irregularity of texture and a coarseness to the touch which can be very appealing. However, it will not cover your canvas as well as some of the other threads. Linen is spun from a long, very straight plant staple that reacts to dye differently than does cotton fiber. The resulting colors of linen floss have a definite muted quality and may have a tendency to rub off because the dye remains on the surface of the thread.

Swedish Kulört Lingarn and English Knox Linen (the shinier of the two) are common brands of linen floss. Both are one strand of 2-ply and may be purchased in small skeins.

Silk: Silk floss is used for the finest needlework. It must be worked on a soft fabric by smooth hands in order to prevent catches. Needlework done with silk floss is exceptionally beautiful, for the colors are vibrant and the sheen is unmatched by any other embroidery floss. However, silk is fairly difficult to work and great care must be taken when handling it.

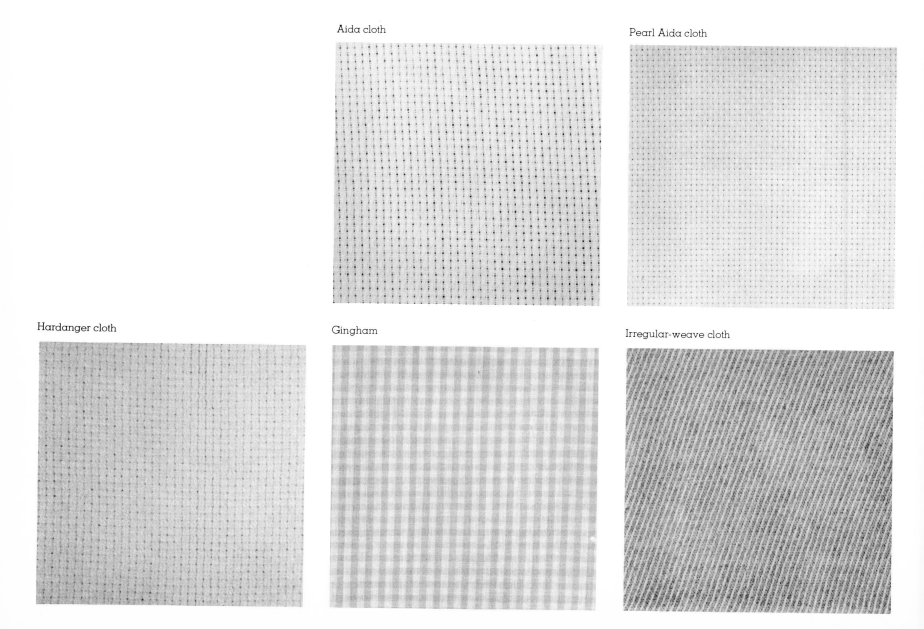

Aida cloth

Pearl Aida cloth

Hardanger cloth

Gingham

Irregular-weave cloth

Cloth

Aida (or Ida) Cloth: Aida cloth is manufactured in Europe especially for cross-stitching. It is woven in a variation of the basket-weave which locks groups of threads together in small, even squares. As a group of four threads is pulled together, both horizontally and vertically, small holes are formed at the corners of the squares. These holes provide a perfect guide for placing the needle; consequently, a cross-stitch that is worked on this cloth will always have a neat, even appearance. Regular Aida cloth is woven from cotton thread and is available in beige, natural, and white, with 8 squares to the inch. A coarse version of Aida cloth is known as Binca cloth and is woven in England.

Pearl Aida Cloth: Pearl Aida cloth resembles regular Aida cloth except for the size of the squares. Pearl Aida has 10 to 12 squares to the inch.

Some Pearl Aida, woven in the Phillipines, comes in beautiful, bright colors—red, yellow, blue, and white. However, since the cloth is not square (one square horizontally equals one and a half squares vertically), it should not be used for anything but abstract and geometric patterns. Be sure to purchase the square Pearl Aida for the projects in this book.

Hardanger: Hardanger, or Monk's cloth as it is sometimes called, is simply a basket-weave fabric that is well-suited for cross-stitch and other forms of even-weave embroidery. The corner holes, however, are not as easily distinguished as are the holes in Aida cloth. It is woven primarily in beige and white, but can sometimes be found in other colors. It is most available in finer meshes* (approximately 22 squares per inch) and is used for more delicate work.

Coarser cloth of a similar type may be found at a few specialty stores (see "Suppliers"). This cloth has fewer squares per inch (usually 8), enabling a pattern to quickly materialize on it. It is available in white, beige, red, dark blue, and ocher.

Linen: Linen has an even-weave and a slightly irregular surface texture. It is available in a variety of colors and a wide range of threads per inch. Linen is traditionally used in Scandinavian thread-count embroidery, where the threads that form the squares on which the stitches are based are individually counted by eye.

Gingham: Cotton gingham has color squares woven directly into the fabric. Since gingham is so finely woven, the corners of the squares may lack definition. Therefore, extra care should be exercised when inserting the needle into each corner. It is easier to work on this fabric if you first baste a lightweight piece of white cotton to the back, giving the gingham a little extra body.

Irregular-weave Fabric: Irregular-weave* fabric, as implied by the name, does not have an equal number of threads warp* to weft* (vertical to horizontal) per inch. When stitching on these fabrics, use scrim as described on page 16.

Canvas

Interlock canvas

Double-thread canvas

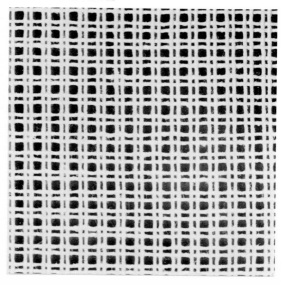

Interlock Canvas: Interlock canvas is woven from cotton threads evenly spaced in both horizontal and vertical directions. The open spaces between the threads form the mesh over which needlepoint is worked. If you examine interlock canvas closely, you will see that each warp and weft thread is formed by two threads that are twisted around each other as they are woven. This twisting makes interlock canvas stronger than mono canvas, another single-mesh canvas. Interlock canvas does not easily lose its shape. It is preferred in the United States over double-threaded (Penelope) canvas because the single hole is easier to see.

When buying canvas, it is always important to buy the best quality. Think of the disappointment in finding, after hours of stitching, that your canvas did not hold its shape and your design is out of line. Look for a canvas with evenly spaced, flawless threads (no lumps or knots), and a polished, semistiff finish. The finish will make the canvas easier to work on and will also prevent the yarn from catching on the canvas threads.

The gauge of any canvas is measured by the number of openings, or meshes, to the inch. Interlock canvas is available in white or ecru, in 10, 12, or 14 mesh. It is woven in widths from 24 to 36 inches, although you may find it cut into smaller widths.

Mono Canvas: Mono canvas is woven from evenly spaced, single threads. The threads are held in place only by the plain weave* and the sizing in the canvas; therefore, mono canvas does not hold its shape very well. Although it may sometimes be less expensive than another canvas, it is not suggested for any of the patterns in this book.

If you do stitch on mono canvas, use only the continental stitch. The stitches used in the half-cross method will slip right through the canvas threads.

Double-Thread (or Penelope) Canvas: Double-thread canvas is woven from pairs of threads that form evenly spaced, alternately large and small meshes in both directions. Except for petit point*, only the large holes are used. The double threads give the canvas added strength and durability. Rug canvas should always be of this type.

Double-thread canvas comes in white or ecru; in 3, 4, 5, 10, 12, 16, and 24 meshes per inch.

Needles

Scrim: Double-thread canvas that is woven with blue thread in every fifth pair of warp threads is called scrim. This canvas is used for stitching over irregular-weave fabrics. Scrim is available in 7 through 15 meshes to the inch.

This is the correct way to use scrim: Cut the scrim slightly larger (at least one inch in each direction) than the fabric on which you plan to stitch. Align the squares of the scrim with the weave of your fabric. Baste the scrim to the fabric along each edge and diagonally across the piece. Stitch the design over the scrim, being careful that each stitch goes through the fabric underneath. Do not catch the scrim with your thread. When you have completed stitching, dampen the scrim with water and carefully pull the individual threads of the scrim from under the stitching. The horizontal threads should be removed before the vertical threads.

Embroidery (Crewel) Needles: At first glance, embroidery needles appear to be similar to the familiar sharps that are used in plain sewing. However, on close inspection, you will notice that an embroidery needle has a longer eye to accommodate the different thicknesses of embroidery threads. Embroidery needles come in assorted sizes which are numbered 1, 2, 3, 4, 5, 7, 9, and 11. A number 1 needle is the largest; an 11 the smallest. Embroidery needles are used specifically for embroidery needlework.

Tapestry Needles: Tapestry needles are larger than embroidery needles. They have a wide, elongated eye which is smooth on the inside so that the yarn or thread will not wear as you stitch. Tapestry needles also have a blunt point which easily slides through even-weave fabric and will not puncture threads. They are packaged in assorted sizes numbered from 14 to 26; 26 being the smallest, 14 the largest.

Accessories: Hoops and frames are used to hold the fabric or canvas taut while you are working. Use of either is entirely optional. It is convenient to have a well-organized carrier for your yarns and threads. Persian wool is often arranged on a small wooden palette that is available in most needlepoint stores; or wool may be kept in a canvas case which can be rolled up neatly and stored when not in use. The yarns are held in place by a ribbon stitched down at regular intervals. A small pocket at the bottom holds needles, scissors, and, if you like, a thimble. Smaller skeins of wool and embroidery flosses may be stored in small baskets or boxes. Empty candy boxes, in particular, work especially well. Other helpful items include a small pair of scissors with a sharp, straight point (to cut yarn), a tape measure or ruler, and a thimble.

Stitches

The continental stitch is a diagonal stitch laid across the thread or threads which form the sides of the mesh in your canvas. When worked in consecutive rows, this stitch completely covers the canvas on both sides; consequently, it is an extremely strong stitch. Use it when the object you are making must withstand heavy wear (for example, a chair seat, handbag, or rug).

The continental stitch may be worked on mono, interlock, or double-thread canvas.

To work the continental stitch, follow Figures 1 and 2. Work the first row from right to left and then invert your canvas to work the next row from right to left again. Follow this procedure for each row.

1. Start at lower right corner. Bring needle out at A, insert at B, and bring out at C; continue, ending row by inserting at B.
2. Invert canvas; bring needle out at A, repeat step 1.

Fig. 1

Fig. 2

Basket-weave Stitch

The basket-weave stitch looks nearly identical to the continental and half-cross stitch on the front side of the canvas; however, the stitch pattern on the back side is different. Because the back is fully covered, as with the continental stitch, these two stitches have similar padding and can be used together or interchangeably. The basket-weave is a very sturdy stitch and has one main virtue—it usually will not distort the canvas. However, it is a more complicated stitch to learn. The basket-weave stitch may be worked on mono, interlock, or double-thread canvas.

To work the basket-weave stitch, follow Figures 1-4. Note that this stitch is worked on the diagonal, but you do not invert the canvas to begin a new row.

1. Start in upper right corner. Bring needle out at A, insert at B, bring out at C. Holding needle vertically, insert at D, bring out at E.
2. Insert needle at F, bring out at G.
3. Holding needle horizontally, insert at H, bring out at I. Continue diagonally up row, with needle in horizontal position.
4. At end of row, bring needle out at J. Holding needle vertically, insert needle at K, bring out at L. Insert needle at M, bring out at N, holding needle vertically. Continue diagonally down row with needle in vertical position. Repeat from Step 2.

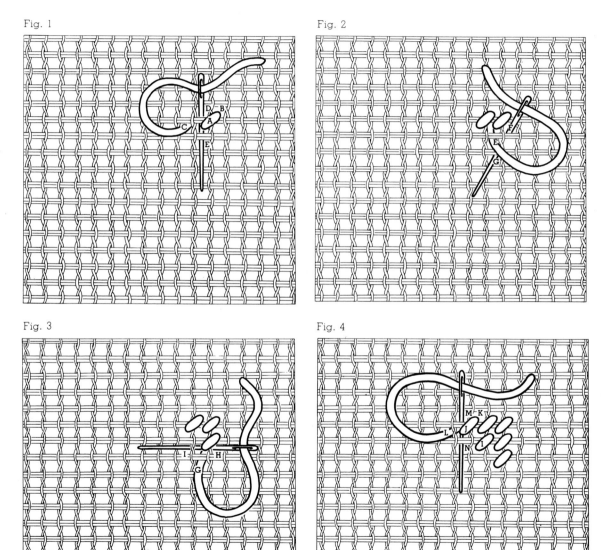

Fig. 1

Fig. 2

Fig. 3

Fig. 4

Half-cross Stitch

On the front side of a needlepoint canvas, both the half-cross and the continental stitch look the same. Only the back of the canvas shows a difference. The half-cross stitch is faster to work, uses less wool, and produces a less-padded canvas. It may be used on interlock or double-thread canvas.

To work the half-cross stitch, follow Figures 1 and 2.

1. Start first row from lower left corner. Bring needle out at A, insert at B, bring out at C. Continue across row from left to right, ending row by inserting at B.

2. Second row: Bring needle out at D, insert at E, bring out at F. Continue across row, working right to left. Third row: Repeat Step 1.

Fig. 1

Fig. 2

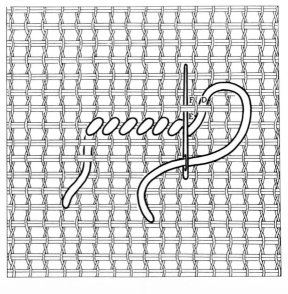

Cross-Stitch

The cross-stitch is composed of two half-cross stitches worked one over the other from opposing corners. It is used in needlepoint for variation of surface texture, and it covers the canvas completely. Cross-stitch is used most often in even-weave embroidery. Depending on the thickness of the yarn or thread and the size of the square on which you are working, the cross-stitch may or may not fully cover the square. Note that all the patterns in this book were designed for a cross-stitch that covers the square.

To work the cross-stitch, follow Figures 1–3.
1. Start first row at lower left corner. Bring needle out at A, insert at B, bring out at C. Continue across row, working left to right, and end by inserting at B.
2. To complete cross, work same row from right to left, crossing over all stitches previously made.
3. Second row: Bring needle out at D, insert at E, and bring out at F. Continue across row as in steps 1 and 2.

Fig. 1

Fig. 2

Fig. 3

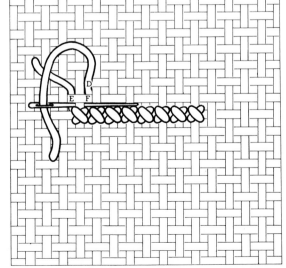

French Knot

The French knot is a curious stitch that makes a knot on the surface of your cloth. It is used in both free and even-weave embroidery for eyes, flower centers, and other special textures.

To work the French knot, follow the figure below.
1. Bring needle out at A. Wind thread over needle two or three times.
2. Insert needle close to, but not in, A. Pull needle through cloth while other hand holds twists in place to form knot on surface.

Outline Stitch

The outline stitch is helpful in adding extra accent to a shape or for separating two similar colors.

To work the outline stitch, follow the figure below.
1. Work from left to right. Bring needle out at end of line to be covered. Insert needle a short distance to the right and then bring out a little way to the left at a slight angle. For even stitches, keep thread above needle.
2. Follow same procedure along design outline.

Backstitch

The backstitch, like the outline stitch, is used to form lines and outlines.

To work the backstitch, follow the figure below.
1. Work from right to left. Bring needle out a short distance from start of line to be covered; insert at start of line (A) and bring out an equal distance ahead along line.
2. Insert needle at start of line and again bring out an equal distance ahead along line. Continue along in this manner.

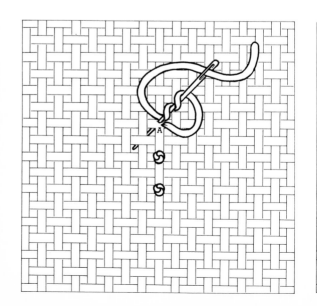

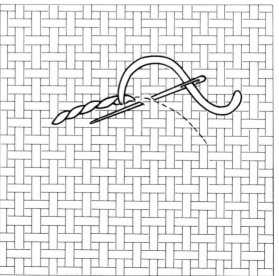

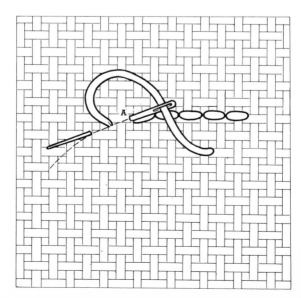

Patterns

General Procedures

Guidelines: The first two projects preceding the series of patterns in the book are designed to give basic step-by-step instructions for transferring and working patterns on Aida cloth and canvas. Directions for blocking and finishing are also given here. Refer to this basic information to accomplish any of the patterns in this book.

For those who want guidelines to follow, each pattern includes a color key and stitch technique. These suggestions should not limit your own creative expression. Feel free to design alternate color schemes and explore all materials and stitches.

The cross-stitch is advised for use on Aida cloth only. The sampler is created by leaving the background unstitched, allowing the texture of the cloth to serve as a field for the design. The continental, half-cross, and basket-weave stitches are for use on needlepoint canvas, where the entire background is covered with stitches. The French knot, outline, and backstitch are used for accents only.

A glossary of needlepoint-related terms appears in the back of the book. An asterisk appearing beside a word in the text indicates that the term is explained in the glossary.

Color Key: A color key accompanies each pattern in the book. The numbers beside each color are keyed to a printed chart (W201) for DMC cotton embroidery floss. If you find the color names in the key too ambiguous, you can purchase this chart at a needlework store or order it directly from the DMC Corporation, 107 Trumbull Street, Elizabeth, N.J. 07206. You may use the chart as a guide to find the exact color of Persian or rug wool, as well. Simply take the chart to your local store and match the numbered colors with the colors in their stock. Then, you can use whatever brands of thread or yarn that are available in your area.

You will note that in many patterns the color-key symbol is repeated more than once. In each case, the specific area to be stitched is indicated, i.e., mouth, eyes, etc. Be sure to read the entire key before beginning your project.

If you wish to experiment with other colors, I suggest that you make a tracing of the pattern and then color it with crayons or colored pencils.

Estimating Cloth or Canvas: To determine the amount of cloth or canvas you will need to work up any of the following patterns, count the number of squares in the pattern (in each direction if it is a 2-page spread, all other patterns are square), and divide by the number of squares per inch in your cloth or canvas. This will give you the number of inches of material you will need to work the pattern. To help facilitate your counting, every tenth square in the pattern is marked by a heavier rule. Be sure to buy at least four extra inches in length and width to allow for fold-over in mounting or for other applications.

Estimating Yarn: In some projects, you will be supplied with yarn amounts. However, since packaging varies so greatly from store to store and brand to brand, it is best to make your own estimates and then purchase accordingly. One way to estimate the yarn you will need to complete a canvas is to work one 10 x 10 square, carefully noting how much yarn is used. Multiply this figure by the number of 10 x 10 squares to be worked in that color to find the required yardage. Or, better yet, seek the advice of an experienced shopkeeper who can help you estimate yarn amounts.

Testing for Colorfastness: It is imperative that both your wool and the marking pen that is used to transfer a pattern to canvas be colorfast. Even those pens that are marked "indelible" should be tested in this manner: Simply mark a scrap of yarn and then wash it in lukewarm water and gentle soapsuds (as in blocking). If the pen bleeds, don't use it! To test wools for colorfastness, wrap some colored scraps in a damp cloth and enclose them in plastic for four or five hours. If the colors run, do not use the wool.

Tips for stitching: The following suggestions will help your stitching move along more easily.

Thread the needle by flattening the end of the thread or yarn between your lips and then slipping it through the eye. Or, fold or wrap the thread around the needle, press the needle against the fold, and slip the needle out. Then press the eye down on the flattened fold. The thread should pop through.

The number of strands to use in your needle is dependent on the weight of the yarn or thread and the size of the fabric mesh. The area of the fabric you are stitching should be totally covered by your stitches, so experiment by taking a few stitches to determine the appropriate number of strands needed. As a rule of thumb, use four strands of 6-strand embroidery floss when working on Pearl Aida. If you are covering a large area with a dark color, you may want to add another strand.

Use short lengths, 10 to 15 inches, of yarn or thread. This will prevent your thread from twisting and knotting up. If you are using several strands of Persian wool, cut your strands twice as long and use half your total number of strands, doubling the strands back on themselves (two strands doubled equal four strands). This will eliminate a double thickness of yarn at the needle's eye and make stitching easier.

When starting a new length of yarn, let 1 to 2 inches of thread hang loose in the back. Catch this piece of thread three times as you work, with every other stitch. Neatly cut off the excess.

To eliminate unnecessary lumps on the back of your fabric, end each new thread by running it under every other stitch (previously worked) three times. Never pull two threads through the same group of stitches.

Try to maintain an even pull on the thread. This will give you a more even stitch quality. Untwist the thread as you work, so that the thickness of the thread does not vary (a twisted thread becomes thinner).

You will find it easier to work in the middle of your canvas if you roll the sides back like a scroll.

To rip out stitches, begin with the last stitch worked and carefully pull out each stitch in reverse order. It is helpful to cut off the unraveled thread after removing every few stitches. Or, you may also clip each stitch with a pair of sharp, pointed scissors and remove the thread with pointed (jeweler's) tweezers. Remove the continental stitch on the wrong side of the canvas; the half-cross on the right side.

To rethread an unraveled piece of yarn, cut out a small piece of paper and fold it around the end of the yarn. Use the paper to slip the yarn through the eye of the needle.

If you are left-handed, read the stitch diagrams upside-down and reverse all instructions.

Little Tommy Tucker
Sings for his supper:
What shall we give him?
White bread and butter.
How shall he cut it
Without e'er a knife?
How will he be married
Without e'er a wife?

- ⊡ Red, 666
- ⊡ Yellow, 444
- ⊿ Green, 905
- ⊠ Blue, 798
- ◩ Black, 310
- ⊞ Rust, 918
- ■ Brown, 436
- ■ Flower centers, Orange, 947
- ■ Boy's eyes, Blue, 798
- □ Eyes, Snow White
- ⊞ Skin tone, 676, 434, 754, 760 or Ecru Outline stitch in shirt, socks, hand, Black, 310

Suggested technique: cross-stitch
Suggested applications: framed wall piece, pillow, clothing, quilt

Basic Project 1: How to Work a Pattern on Aida cloth
Little Tommy Tucker, a framed wall piece

Grid size: 111 x 111 squares
Stitch: cross-stitch
Materials: 10-squares-per-inch Pearl
Aida cloth, cut 15 x 15 inches
Cotton embroidery floss: 3 skeins each of
bright red, bright blue, bright green,
bright yellow; 1 skein each of snow
white, orange, black, dark brown, red
brown, skin tone or ecru
#7 embroidery needle
Ruler
Soft pencil
Scissors
1-inch-wide masking tape (optional)
Thread for basting
Towel
Wooden or composition board for
blocking
Contact paper
Rustproof tacks
Framing materials: 12 x 12-inch plywood
backing board, staples or tacks,
12 x 12-inch frame, matting (optional)

Procedure: The best way to transfer a pattern to Aida cloth is to make a grid on your cloth that corresponds to the one on the pattern. To do this, count the number of horizontal and vertical squares in the pattern (every group of 10 squares is marked by a heavier rule). In this pattern there are 111 squares horizontally and vertically. These are arranged in 11 groups of 10 squares. (You will note that in the Tommy Tucker pattern there is one additional row of squares along the top and right-hand sides.) You should

carefully count groups of squares in each pattern in the book before marking Aida cloth.

Lay an ample piece of Pearl Aida cloth flat on a table, making sure that one of the two cut edges is cut perfectly straight. As you face the fabric, place the straight cut edge on the left, with the selvage* edges running along the top and bottom. Measure in 2 inches from the lower left-hand corner in both horizontal and vertical directions and make a mark with a soft pencil along each edge of the cloth. From each of these two pencil marks, measure 11 inches with a ruler (remembering that Pearl Aida cloth has 10 squares to the inch), or count 11 groups of 10 small squares. Mark each inch, or group of 10 squares, with a soft pencil along the very edge of the fabric. Now measure another 2 inches beyond the pattern area and cut your fabric along these lines. Your cut fabric should be 15 x 15 inches (2 inches plus 11 inches plus 2 inches equals 15 inches). To prevent the edges of your cloth from fraying, use an overcast stitch* or masking tape to bind the raw edges (Fig. 1). Next, with your basting thread and a simple running stitch, make lines through your fabric which correspond to the heavy lines in the pattern (Fig. 2). This basting thread grid will enable you to reconstruct the design, square by square, as indicated on the pattern. By stitching each 10 x 10 group of squares individually, the changes of major errors in your finished piece will be greatly reduced.

With four strands of embroidery floss in your needle, start working in the lower left-hand corner of your basting thread grid. Begin with cross-stitching the flower border. Follow the color changes indicated by the different textures keyed to the pattern. Next stitch in Little Tommy from the feet up. Outline the large areas of color in the half-cross stitch and then fill them in. Stitch in the eyes, mouth, and buttons before filling in the face and shirt areas. Outline the apple, stitch in the name, fill in the apple, and add the leaf and stem. Lastly, to define the shape of the legs and arms, use the outline stitch in black or dark brown.

When you have finished stitching, carefully remove the basting threads from the fabric. Do not remove the tape or stitching from the edges. Lightly agitate the fabric in lukewarm water and gentle soapsuds. Rinse fabric well and roll up in a towel to remove excess water (do not wring or squeeze).

To block, stretch the fabric on a wooden or composition board that you have covered on one side with Contact paper (the Contact paper prevents the wood from staining your fabric). Using rustproof tacks, secure each corner, pulling the fabric taut and square as you work. Next, tack the middle of each side, and place tacks at 2-inch intervals all the way around (see Fig. 3). When your fabric is thoroughly dry, remove the tacks and the edge bindings. You are now ready to frame your finished Tommy Tucker.

Consider carefully how you will frame your stitching, for it is the finished presentation that makes your work look neat and professional. Visit a frame shop and don't hesitate to ask a framer for advice. Here are two suggestions for framing: 1) Purchase a 12 x 12-inch Plexiglas frame with a depth of 1¼ inches. Cut a piece of plywood approximately 12 x 12 inches to fit inside the frame. Wrap your cross-stitch around the board, tacking or stapling the fabric to the back and neatly mitering* the corners (see Fig. 4). Slip the mounted cross-stitch into the frame. 2) Purchase a plain ¼- or ½-inch silver frame with inside dimensions of 18 x 18½ inches. Choose a blue matte that matches your stitching. Have the frame store cut it to a 3½-inch border on the top and sides, and a 4-inch border on the bottom. If you wish, add a ⅛-inch-wide, secondary yellow matte under the blue matte. Have the framer mount your cross-stitch and complete the framing.

Fig. 1

Fig. 2

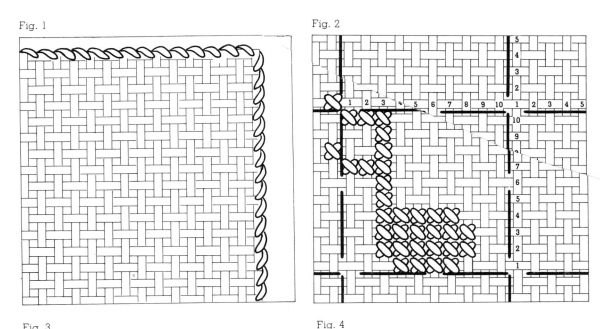

Fig. 3

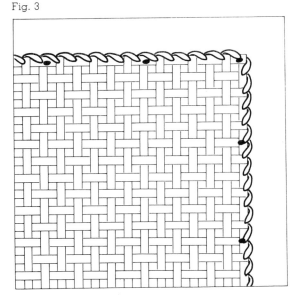

Fig. 4

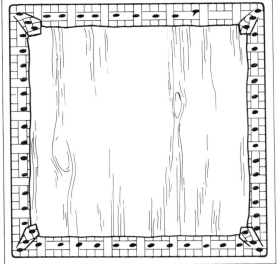

Basic Project 2: How to Work a Pattern on Canvas
Little Miss Muffet
A pillow

Grid size: 99 x 99 squares
Stitch: continental
Materials: 10 squares-per-inch interlock canvas, cut 14 x 14 inches
Colorfast Persian wool: 4 ounces ecru, 2 ounces gray blue, 1 ounce each of yellow green, light yellow, lavender, gold, skin tone or ecru; 1 strand dark pink for mouth; 2 strands gray for oatmeal and spoon; 2 strands light blue for bowl; 2 strands black for shoes
#8 tapestry needle
Scissors
1-inch-wide masking tape
Colorfast marking pen
10 squares-per-inch graph paper or photostat of pattern
Wax crayons (optional)
½ yard of blue fabric in color that harmonizes with gray blue yarn
7-inch-long blue zipper
10 x 10-inch muslin pillow filled with down or Dacron
Towel
Plastic bag
Wooden or composition board for blocking
Contact paper
Rustproof tacks
Straight pins
Sewing machine (optional)
Soft cording (optional)

Procedure: The traditional way to transfer a pattern to canvas is to duplicate the design freehand, square by square, using a colorfast marker. Note that the pattern will be transposed onto the threads of the canvas, as opposed to the squares of Aida cloth (see Fig. 1). Do not count the canvas holes, or meshes*, as this will only confuse your count. Since the traditional method of counting squares can be somewhat tedious, we suggest you try one of the following two alternate methods. On graph paper with the same number of squares per inch as your canvas—in this case, 10 squares per inch—redraw the design with a fairly heavy black line. Then lay your canvas over the graph paper and, with a colorfast marker, trace the design onto the canvas.

A quicker and easier but more expensive way to transfer the pattern is to have a local printer shoot a photostat, or velox, of the pattern design, using the same number of squares per inch as on your canvas. Simply ask the cameraman to enlarge one group of 10 squares to the same size as 10 squares on your canvas. Be sure to ask him to use a non-shrink or resin-coated paper. Then lay your canvas over the photostat and, using a colorfast marker, trace the design onto the canvas. If you prefer to work on a colored surface, you may color in the design areas of the canvas with crayons that match your wool as closely as possible. When you have finished, place the canvas between two pieces of paper and run a hot iron over the top paper to smooth out the colors.

Once you have transferred the design, secure the raw edges of the canvas with either masking tape, an overcast stitch*, or a loose, machine zig-zag stitch. This will keep your canvas neat while you work.

Thread your needle with three strands of two-ply Persian wool. Using the continental stitch, complete the gray blue in the border. Then fill in all the other color areas, saving the ecru background for last. Run one extra row of dark blue stitches around the outer edge of the border.

After you have completed stitching Miss Muffet, block the canvas. In blocking, there is just one principle to remember—you want to wet the sizing on the canvas, without washing it away. To block your canvas, wet a towel and wring out the excess water. Roll up your canvas in the towel and then wrap the roll in a plastic bag. Let it stand for four or five hours. Then, using rustproof tacks, secure the canvas to a wooden or composition board that you have covered on one side with Contact paper. Pull the canvas into shape as you tack and be sure not to drive the tacks through the threads of the canvas, as this will weaken and possibly break them. When your canvas has dried completely, remove it, undo the edge bindings, and trim down the borders to one inch.

To make the pillow backing, cut the blue fabric to the same size as your blocked canvas—in this case, 12 x 12 inches. If you wish to add piping to your pillow, read final paragraph before continuing. With right sides facing, pin the two pieces together. Using a machine basting stitch, make a 1-inch seam on one side. Sew the closed zipper into this seam, following instructions on the package for a center opening (see Fig. 2). Remove the machine basting and open the zipper. Again making a 1-inch seam, stitch the remaining three sides of the pillow, continuing around the fourth side to meet the ends of the zipper opening (see Fig. 3). Clip the corners. Turn the pillowcase right side out and insert your muslin pillow.

If you are an experienced sewer, you might wish to trim your pillow with piping. You can either purchase piping, or make it from leftover fabric. To make piping, piece together 3-inch-wide strips of bias from the blue fabric. Then fold the pieced strip, right side out, over soft cording and, using a zipper foot, machine-stitch as closely as possible to the cording. Pin your piping to the right side of your needlepoint canvas so that the corded edge faces the center of the canvas, and so that the stitching next to the cording aligns with the seam line on the canvas. Baste the piping in place by stitching along the seam line, on top of the stitching next to the cord (see Fig. 4). Refer to previous paragraph for final instructions.

Fig. 1

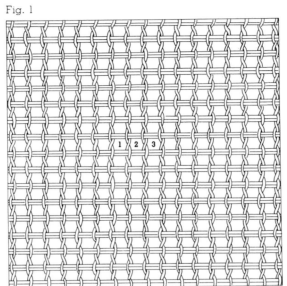

Fig. 2

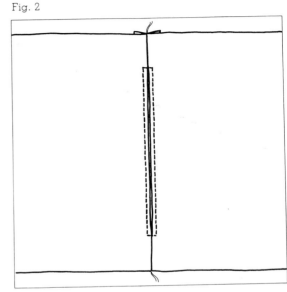

Fig. 3

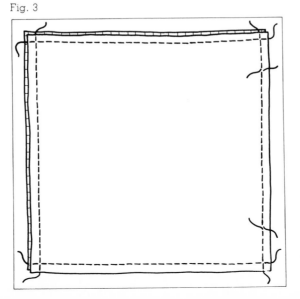

Fig. 4

Little Miss Muffet
Sat on a tuffet,
Eating her curds and whey;
There came a big spider,
Who sat down beside her
And frightened Miss Muffet
away.

■ Gray blue, 792
□ Ecru
☒ Yellow Green, 472
⊡ Yellow, 444
⊙ Gold, 740
⊞ Lavender, 554
☐ Skin tone, 676, 434, 754, 760 or
  Ecru
☑ Light Blue, 799
⫿ Gray, 414
◪ Black, 310
■ Mouth, Dark Pink, 603

Outline stitch for spider string,
  Yellow Green, 472
Outline stitch for legs, neck,
  Gray Blue, 792

Suggested technique: continental stitch or half-cross
Suggested applications: pillow,
framed wall piece, clothing

Little Bo-peep has lost her
    sheep,
And doesn't know where to
    find them;
Leave them alone, and
    they'll come home,
Bringing their tails behind
    them.

☐ Snow White
⊡ Light Blue, 809
■ Rust, 918
⊠ Blue, 798
⊡ Yellow, 444
⊿ Violet, 553
◹ Green, 905
◺ Yellow Green, 907
⊙ Gold, 741
⊞ Skin tone, 676, 434, 754, 760
    or Ecru
■ Mouth, Dark Pink, 603
Outline stitch around collar,
    sheep, Blue, 798
Outline stitch in neck, legs,
    shoes, Rust, 918

Suggested technique:
    cross-stitch
Suggested applications:
    pillow, framed wall piece,
    clothing, quilt

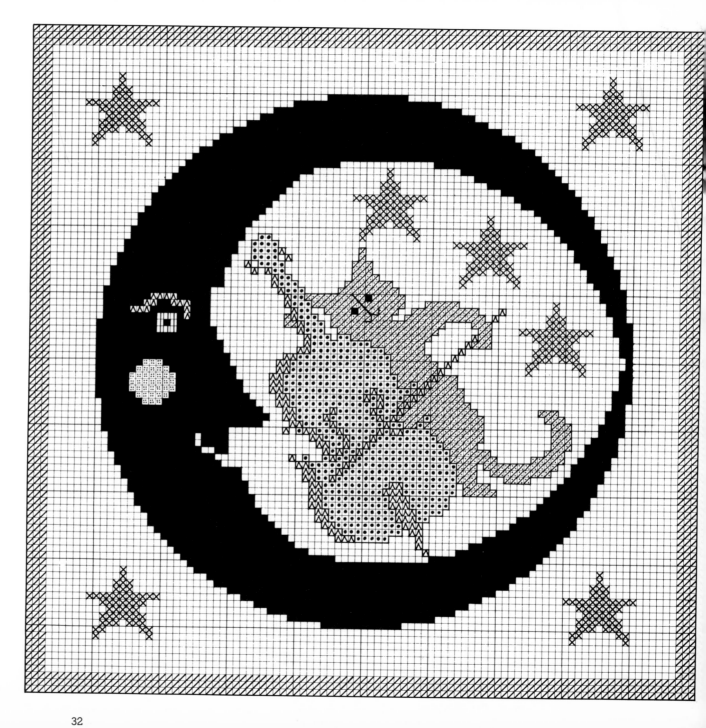

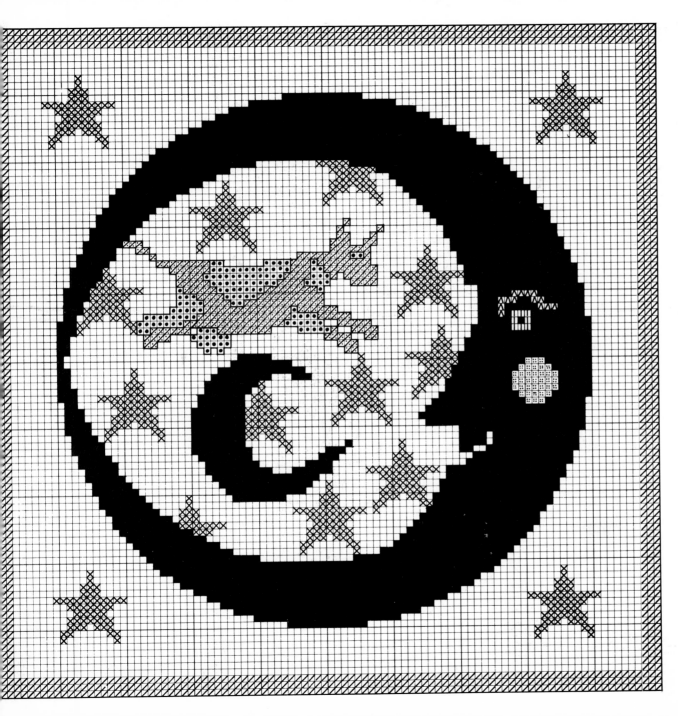

Hey diddle, diddle
The cat and the fiddle,
The cow jumped over
the moon;
The little dog laughed
To see such sport,
And the dish ran away with
the spoon.

⊞ Blue, 519
⊞ Dark Pink, 603
⊠ Yellow, 307
■ Gold, 742
□ Dark Blue, 797
◪ Light Blue, 799
◮ Rust, 918
◉ Tan, 976
◩ Beige, 437
◉ Cow's eye, Dark Blue, 797
■ Cat's eye, Dark Blue, 797
Outline stitch for cat's nose,
Dark Blue, 797

Suggested technique:
half-cross or continental
stitch
Suggested applications:
pillow, framed wall piece

There was an old woman
tossed up in a basket,
Seventeen times as high as
the moon;
Where she was going I
couldn't but ask it,
For in her hand she carried
a broom.

⊡ Light Gray, 415
⊟ Gold, 741
☒ Rust, 918
☑ Tan, 976
◪ Ocher, 783
■ Black, 310
◩ Red, 606
⊙ Red Violet, 917
☐ Light Blue, 809
⊡ Cloud, Snow White
⊡ Skin tone, 676, 434, 754, 760
   or Ecru
Outline stitch in face, Black,
310

Suggested technique:
   half-cross or continental
   stitch
Suggested applications:
   pillow, framed wall piece

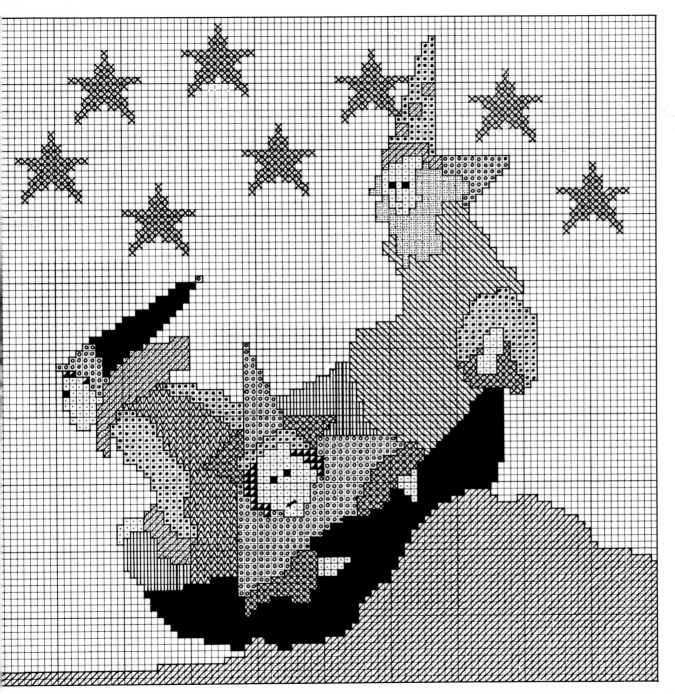

Three wise men of Gotham
Went to sea in a bowl;
If the bowl had been
   stronger
My story would have been
   longer.

⊠ Yellow, 444
⊿ Green, 911
■ Gray Brown, 611
⊡ Light Gray, 415
◩ Purple, 209
⊙ Light Blue, 799
◉ Gold, 740
◮ Red Violet, 917
◪ Brown, 610
⊠ Orange, 947
⊞ Gray, 414
⊡ Skin tone, 676, 434, 754, 760
   or Ecru
Outline stitch in faces, Black,
   310
Optional for half-cross or
   continental stitch only: sky,
   Light Blue, 799

Suggested technique:
   cross-stitch, half-cross, or
   continental stitch
Suggested applications:
   pillow, framed wall piece

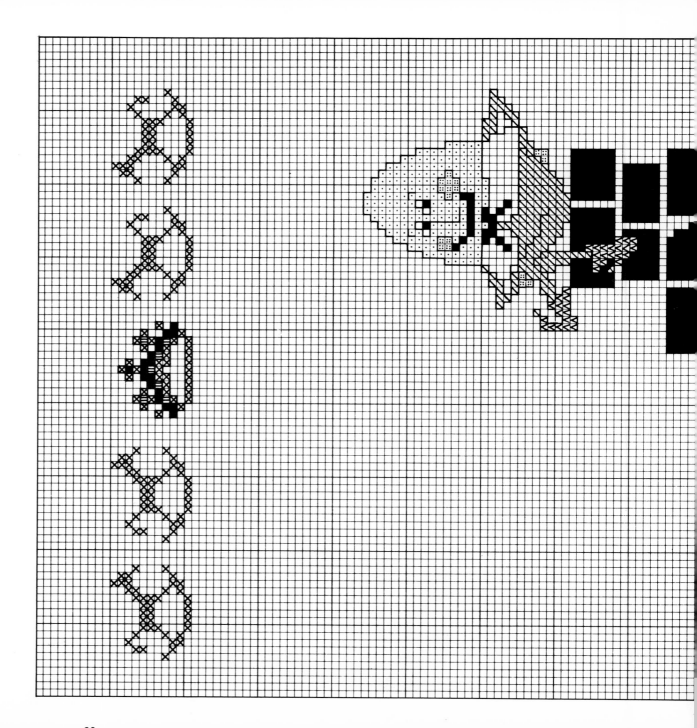

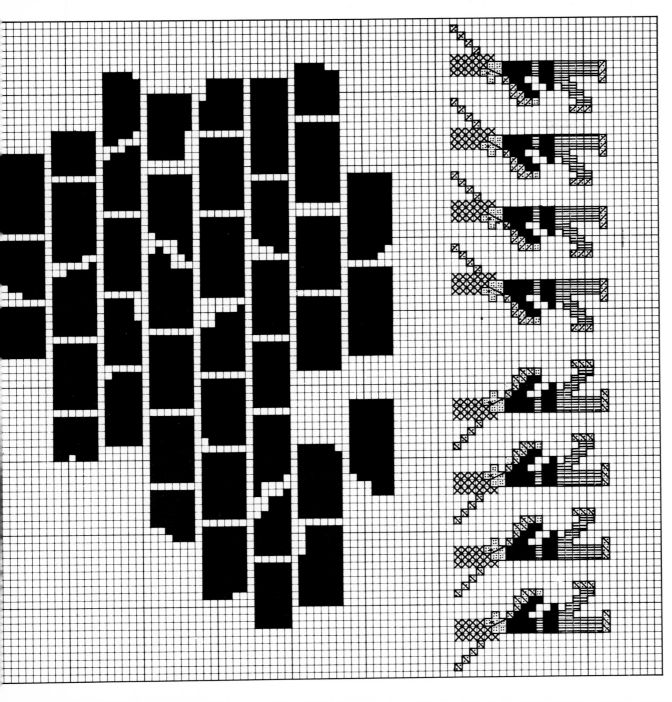

Humpty Dumpty sat on a
wall,
Humpty Dumpty had a
great fall;
All the King's horses and
all the King's men
Couldn't put Humpty
Dumpty together again.

- ■ Red, 606
- ⊠ Dark Blue, 797
- ▥ Green, 905
- ◩ Black, 310
- ▨ Gold, 740
- □ Snow White
- ◩ Brown, 801
- ▥ Peach, 352
- ⊡ Light Yellow, 743
- ■ Humpty Dumpty's eyes, Dark
  Blue, 797

Outline stitch around egg,
  Black, 310
Outline stitch in egg, Black,
  310
French knot for eyes of horses,
  soldiers, Dark Blue, 797
Straight stitch for soldiers' chin
  straps, Dark Blue, 797

Suggested technique:
  cross-stitch
Suggested applications:
  framed wall piece, quilt

A red dot of sun comes up
I follow my master's lead,
He rides a horse through
  the street
And I am on a dragon in
  the sea.

⊠ Yellow Green, 907
■ Green, 905
⊡ Light Peach, 353
⊡ Orange, 947
□ Light Blue, 809
⊞ Blue, 519
⊡ Blue Green, 517
□ Eye, Snow White

Suggested technique:
  cross-stich, half-cross, or
  continental stitch
Suggested applications:
  framed wall piece

Sing a song of sixpence,
A pocket full of rye;
Four and twenty
    blackbirds,
Baked in a pie.

When the pie was opened,
The birds began to sing;
Was not that a dainty dish,
To set before a king?

◉ Black, 310
◨ Red, 606
⊠ Dark Blue, 797
☑ Gold, 741
■ Rust, 918
⊡ Tan, 976
⊠ Brown, 435
⊡ Beige, 437
Half-cross for birds' beaks,
    Gold, 741
French knots for eyes, Gold,
    741

Suggested technique:
    cross-stitch
Suggested applications:
    pillow, framed wall piece,
    clothing, quilt

Plate 1
Little Tommy Tucker,
a framed wall piece

Plate 2
Little Miss Muffet, a pillow

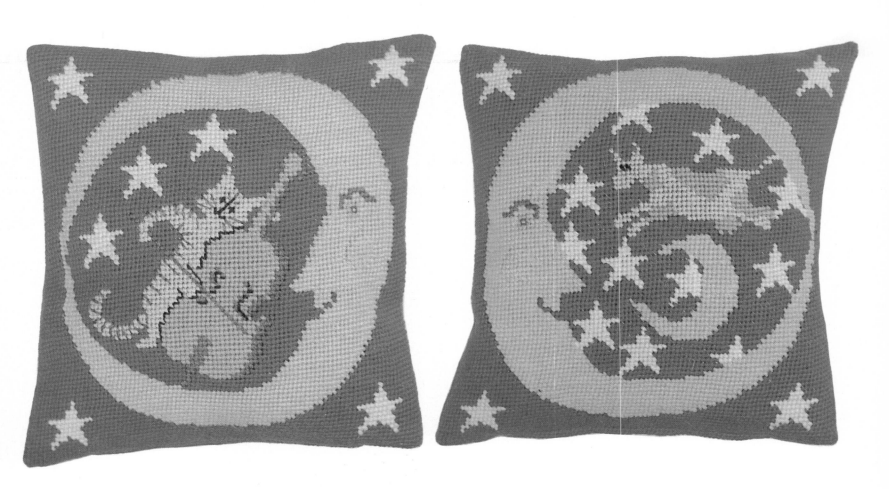

Plate 3
Hey diddle, diddle, two pillows

Plate 4
Hickory, dickory, dock, a clock face

Plate 5
Polly put the kettle on, a tea cozy

Plate 6
Pussy cat, pussy cat, a stuffed toy

Plate 7
Hinx minx, an area rug

Plate 8
Cuckoo, cuckoo, cherry tree
(a family tree), a framed wall piece

Peter, Peter, pumpkin eater,

Had a wife and couldn't
keep her;

He put her in a pumpkin
shell

And there he kept her very
well.

☑ Yellow Green, 907
⊠ Gold, 742
⊡ Green, 905
⊡ Orange, 947
⊠ Yellow, 444
⊞ Dark Blue, 797
Ⅲ Yellow, 444
⊠ Brown, 435
■ Rust, 918

Outline stitch for mouths,
    Black, 310
French knot for eyes, Black, 310
Optional for half-cross
    or continental stitch
    only: background, Ecru

Suggested technique:
    cross-stitch, half-cross, or
    continental stitch
Suggested applications: pillow,
    framed wall piece, clothing,
    quilt

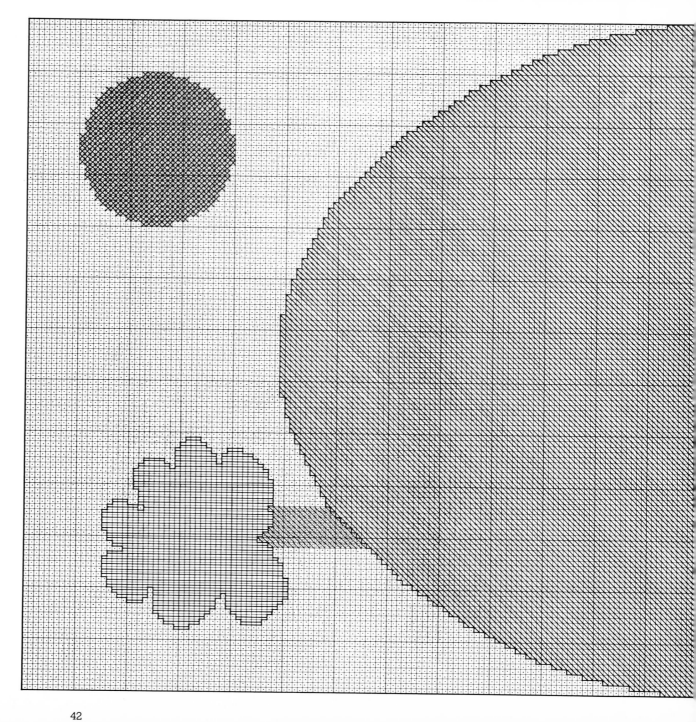

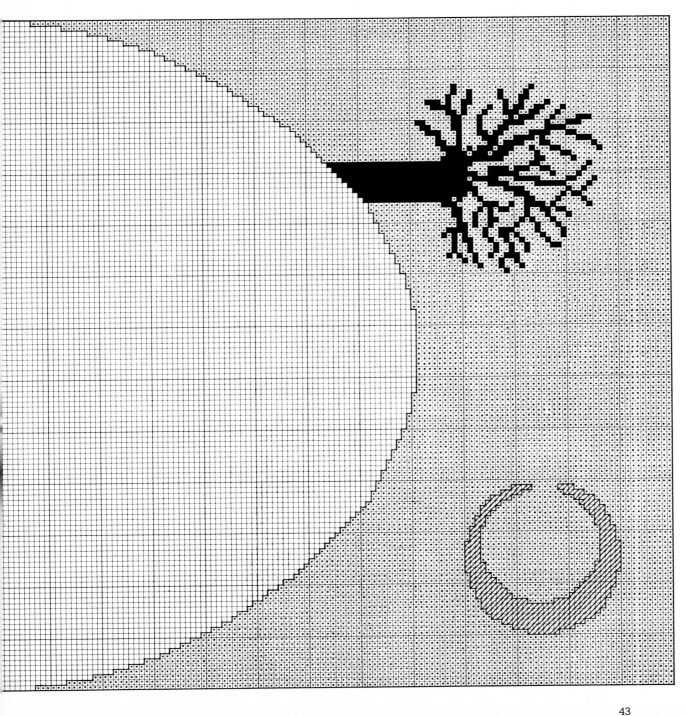

In Spring I look gay,

Decked in comely array,

In Summer more clothing I
   wear;

When colder it grows,

I fling off my clothes

And in Winter quite naked
   appear.

⊠ Orange, 947
☑ Green, 906
⊞ Dark Green, 904
☑ Brown, 610
⊡ Medium Blue, 519
☐ Snow White
◫ Yellow, 444
⊙ Dark Blue, 797
■ Black, 310

Suggested technique: latch
   hooking
Suggested applications: rug

43

Great A, little a,

Bouncing B,

The cat's in the cupboard

And can't see me.

⊡ Pale Blue, 800
⊞ Light Blue, 799
◉ Dark Blue, 797
◪ Red, 606
⊠ Gold, 740
◿ Red Violet, 917
■ Yellow Green, 907
⊡ Brown, 436
◙ Eyes, Blue, 793
Straight stitch for cat's nose,
    Black, 310

Suggested technique:
    cross-stitch
Suggested applications:
    pillow, framed wall piece

Higglety, pigglety, pop!

The dog has eaten the mop;

The pig's in a hurry,

The cat's in a flurry,

Higglety, pigglety, pop!

☑ Light Peach, 353
◪ Pig, Peach, 352
⊙ Black, 310
⊡ Brown, 436
◪ Broom, Rust, 918
⊠ Blue, 793
■ Green, 905
⊞ Tan, 976
■ Dog, pig's eyes, pig's snout,
   Rust, 918
Outline stitch for mop strings,
   Gold, 740
Outline stitch for pig's tail,
   Peach, 352

Suggested technique:
   cross-stitch
Suggested applications:
   pillow, framed wall piece

Snow, snow faster,
Ally-ally-blaster;
The old woman's plucking
   her geese,
Selling the feathers a
   penny a piece.

☑ Light Blue, 799
☐ Dark Blue, 797
⊠ Snow White

Suggested technique: latch
   hooking
Suggested applications: rug

Molly, my sister and I fell
    out,
And what do you think it
    was all about?
She loved coffee and I
    loved tea,
And that was the reason we
    couldn't agree.

■ Dark Blue, 797
☒ Green, 913
□ Light Blue, 799
☒ Dark Pink, 603
◉ Light Yellow, 743
◎ Tan, 976
◪ Gold, 741
⊞ Light Gray, 415
◪ Gray, 451
⊡ Skin tone, 676, 434, 754, 760
    or Ecru
■ Mouth, Dark Pink, 603
Outline stitch around teacups,
    handles, Black, 310
Outline stitch for mouth, Dark
    Pink, 603
Outline stitch in faces, Black,
    310

Suggested technique:
    cross-stitch
Suggested applications:
    pillow, clothing

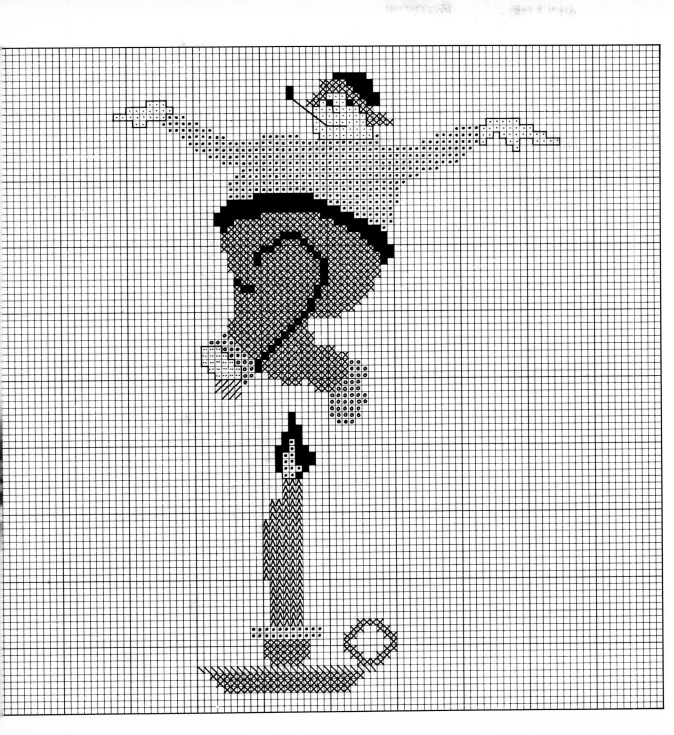

Jack be nimble,
Jack be quick,
Jack jump over
The candlestick.

■ Red, 606
☉ Yellow, 444
◩ Light Blue, 799
⊠ Dark Blue, 797
◪ Green, 905
▨ Gray, 451
⊡ Light Gray, 415
◉ Black, 310
⊡ Skin tone, 676, 434, 754, 760
    or Ecru
■ Eyes, Light Blue, 799
Outline stitch for pipe stem,
    face, Black, 310

Suggested technique:
    cross-stitch
Suggested applications:
    pillow, clothing

Old Mother Goose

When she wanted to
    wander,
Would ride through the air
On a very fine gander.

⊠ Orange, 947
⊘ Gold, 741
⊡ Light Gray, 415
⊡ Snow White
◉ Gray, 451
◙ Red, 606
■ Yellow, 444
⊞ Dark Pink, 603
⊠ Black, 310
⊠ Pink, 604
⊞ Skin tone, 676, 434, 754, 760
    or Ecru
■ Eyes, Black, 310
□ Eyes, Snow White
Outline stitch in face, Black,
    310
Optional for half-cross or
    continental stitch only: sky,
    Light Blue, 799

Suggested technique:
    cross-stitch, half-cross, or
    continental stitch
Suggested applications:
    pillow, framed wall piece,
    clothing, quilt

The greedy man is he who sits
And bites bits out of plates,
Or else takes up an almanac
And gobbles all the dates.

■ Dark Blue, 797
▣ Red, 606
☒ Yellow, 444
⊞ Light Blue, 809
⊡ Snow White
◉ Green, 905
◩ Black, 310
◮ Gold, 741
◪ Hair, Brown, 801
⊡ Skin tone, 676, 434, 754, 760 or Ecru
Outline stitch in shirt, pants, face, Black, 310

Suggested technique:
    cross-stitch
Suggested applications:
    framed wall piece, clothing

Ring-a-ring o' roses,
A pocket full of posies,
A-tishoo! A-tishoo!
We all fall down.

◧ Light Yellow, 743
◪ Peach, 352
⊡ Light Blue, 809
▣ Light Green, 368
✖ Tan, 976
■ Black, 310
⊡ Skin tone, 676
⊞ Skin tone, 754
Ⅲ Dark Blue, 797
✖ Green, 905
Outline stitch in arms, Black,
   310

Suggested technique:
   cross-stitch
Suggested applications:
   pillow, clothing

"No, no, my melodies will
    never die,
While nurses sing, or
    babies cry."
            —Mother Goose, 1833

⊠ Green, 905
⊡ Light Blue, 809
◪ Rust, 918
☐ Snow White
◪ Dark Pink, 603
⊙ Yellow, 444
⊟ Yellow Green, 907
⊞ Light Green, 368
◢ Peach, 352
◉ Orange, 947
⊠ Red, 606
⊡ Gold, 741
◺ Dark Blue, 797
⊡ Skin tone, 676, 434, 754, 760
    or Ecru
■ Brown, 435
■ Eyes, Dark Blue, 797 or Rust,
    918
Outline stitch for mouths, Dark
    Pink, 603
Outline stitch in roof, Black,
    310
Outline stitch in stool, house,
    collar, face, hand, Rust, 918

Suggested technique:
    half-cross or continental
    stitch
Suggested applications:
    pillow, framed wall piece

Cackle, cackle, Mother
    Goose,

Have you any feathers
    loose?

Truly have I, pretty fellow,

Half enough to fill a pillow.

Here are quills, take one or
    two,

And down to make a bed
    for you.

⊞ Beige, 644
◪ Gray Brown, 611
◉ Gold, 741
⊠ Brown, 435
■ Yellow, 444
Ⅲ Red, 606
◉ Dark Blue, 797
⊠ Light Blue, 809
◪ Orange, 947
◪ Green, 905
⊡ Skin tone, 676, 434, 754, 760
    or Ecru
■ Eye, Dark Blue, 797
Outline stitch for mouth, Red,
    606
Outline stitch in boy, Black,
    310

Suggested technique:
    cross-stitch
Suggested applications:
    pillow, clothing

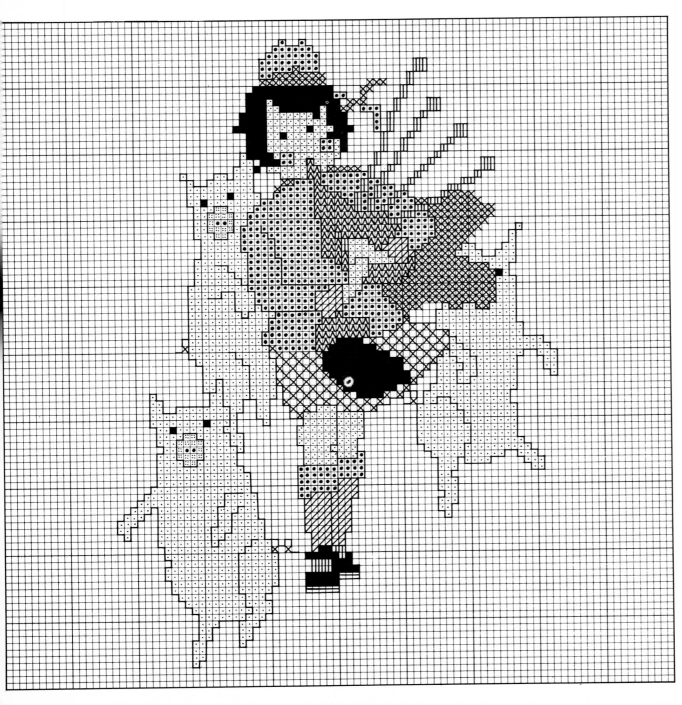

To market, to market, to
    buy a fat pig,
Home again, home again,
    jiggety jig.
To market, to market, to
    buy a fat hog,
Home again, home again,
    jiggety jog.
To market, to market, to
    buy a plum bun,
Home again, home again,
    market is done.

- ⊡ Red, 606
- ⊠ Dark Blue, 797
- ☐ Green, 905
- ⊞ Gold, 741
- ■ Rust, 918
- ◩ Tan, 976
- ◿ Yellow, 444
- ⊟ Black, 310
- ⊡ Light Peach, 353
- ⊞ Peach, 352
- ■ Boy's eyes, Dark Blue, 797
- ⊡ Skin tone, 754

Outline stitch in pigs, Peach,
    352
Outline stitch in boy, Black,
    310
French knot for pigs' snouts,
    Black, 310

Suggested technique:
    cross-stitch
Suggested applications:
    framed wall piece, clothing

Mother Goose Sampler

- ⊠ Green, 701
- ◩ Leaves, Yellow Green, 907
- ▨ Border, Blue, 793
- ■ Blue, 793
- ◪ Red, 666
- ⊡ Gray, 318
- ◲ Light Gray, 415
- ◉ Yellow, 444
- ✖ Orange, 947
- ▱ Gold, 741
- ⊞ Pink, 604

Outline stitch for mouth, Black, 310

Straight stitch for chicks' legs, Black, 310

Half-cross for beaks, Black, 310

French knots for eyes, Black, 310

Suggested technique:
   cross-stitch

Suggested applications:
   framed wall piece

Plate 9
Mother Goose sampler,
a framed wall piece

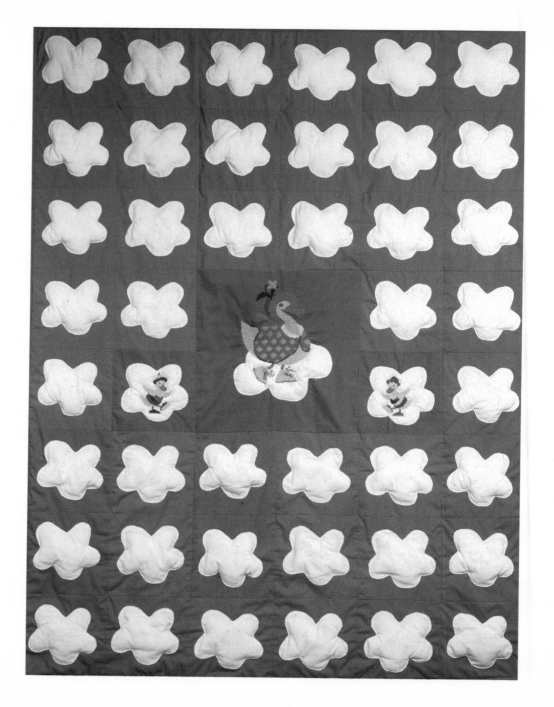

Plate 10
Mother Goose Family, a quilt

Plate 11
There was an old woman who lived in a shoe, a child's smock

Plate 12
Old Mother Goose, a framed wall piece

Old Mother Goose
When she wanted to
  wander,
Would ride through the air
On a very fine gander.

- ⊡ Snow White
- ☐ Light Blue, 799
- ☑ Yellow, 444
- ⊞ Light Gray, 415
- ☒ Gold, 742
- ⊙ Dark Pink, 603
- ■ Dark Blue, 797
- ◩ Green, 905

Outline stitch for rein, Dark
  Blue, 797
Outline stitch for mouth, Dark
  Pink, 603
French knot for eyes, Dark
  Blue, 797

Suggested technique:
  half-cross or continental
  stitch
Suggested applications:
  pillow, framed wall piece

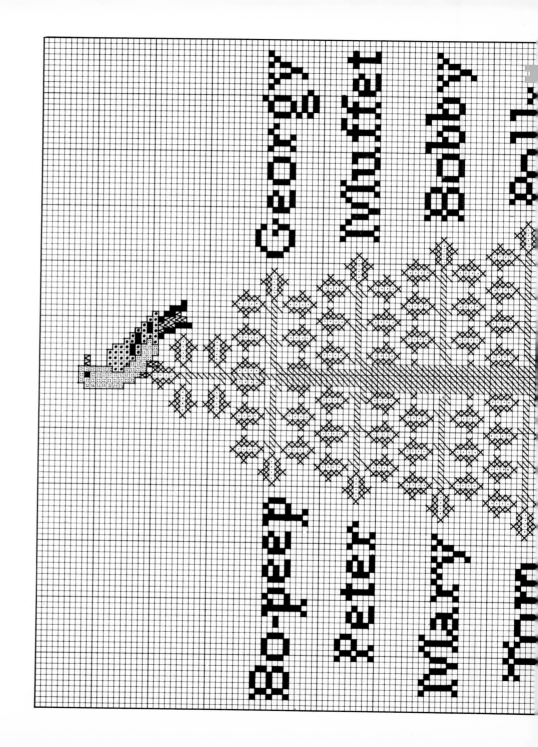

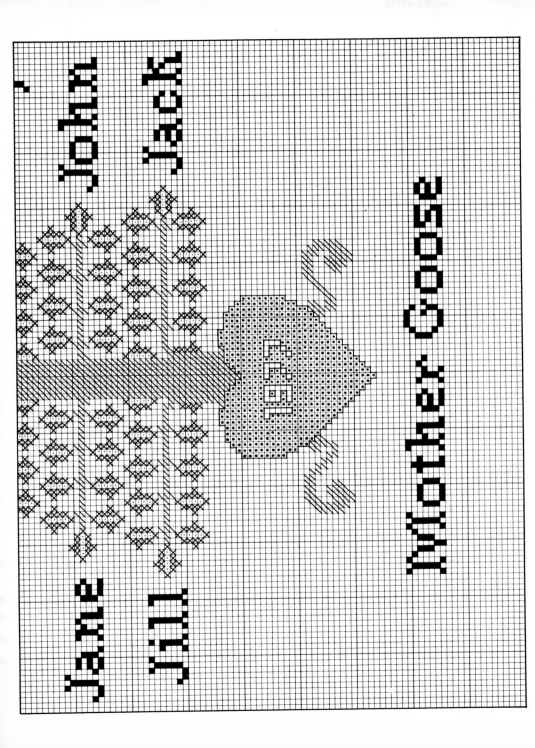

Cuckoo, cuckoo, cherry
  tree,
Catch a bird, and give it to
  me;
Let the tree be high or low,
Let it hail or rain or snow.

- ⊙ Dark Pink, 601
- ■ Blue Green, 826
- ☒ Green, 701
- ⊡ Yellow Green, 907
- ▨ Dark Gray, 844
- ⊞ Yellow, 444
- ◪ Gold, 741

Use letters in sampler on page
  60 to compose your own
  family names.

Suggested technique:
  cross-stitch
Suggested applications:
  framed wall piece

A, B, C, and D,

Pray, playmates, agree.

E, F, and G,

Well, so it shall be.

J, K, and L,

In peace we will dwell.

M, N, and O,

To play let us go.

P, Q, R, and S,

Love may we possess.

W, X, and Y,

Will not quarrel or die.

Z, and ampersand,

Go to school at command.

■ Black, 310

☒ Light Blue, 799

Suggested technique:
    cross-stitch
Suggested applications:
    framed wall piece

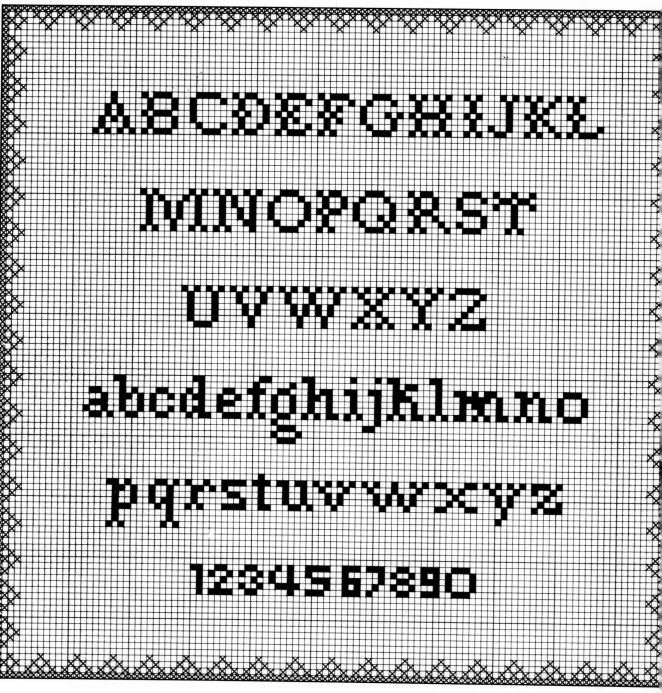

Jack and Jill
Went up the hill,
To fetch a pail of water;
Jack fell down,
And broke his crown,
And Jill came tumbling
    after.

⊡ Light Blue, 809
⊠ Red, 606
□ Green, 905
☑ Yellow Green, 907
⊡ Snow White
■ Peach, 894
⊙ Yellow, 444
◪ Black, 310
◪ Dark Blue, 797
⊞ Light Gray, 415
■ Hair, eyes, Brown, 801
Straight stitch for flower stems,
    Yellow Green, 907
Straight stitch for bucket
    handle, Black, 310
French knot for mouths, Dark
    Pink, 603

Suggested technique:
    half-cross or continental
    stitch
Suggested applications:
    pillow, framed wall piece

March winds and April
   showers
Bring forth May flowers.

☒ Dark Pink, 603
⊡ Light Yellow, 743
⊙ Green, 905
■ Dark Blue, 797
☒ Blue, 806
⊠ Gold, 740

Suggested technique:
   cross-stitch
Suggested applications:
   pillow, framed wall piece

What are little girls made
of, made of?
What are little girls made
of?
Sugar and spice
And all things nice,
That's what little girls are
made of.

- ☒ Red, 606
- ◨ Green, 905
- ▥ Brown, 435
- ■ Gold, 740
- ⊡ Yellow, 444
- ⊡ Pink, 604
- ◉ Light Yellow, 743
- ◣ Violet, 553
- ⊠ Light Blue, 799
- ⊗ Dark Pink, 603
- ⊞ Skin tone, 754

Outline stitch for mouths, Dark
Pink, 603
French knots in strawberries,
Dark Pink, 603
French knots for eyes, Light
Blue, 799, Green, 905

Suggested technique:
cross-stitch
Suggested applications:
framed wall piece

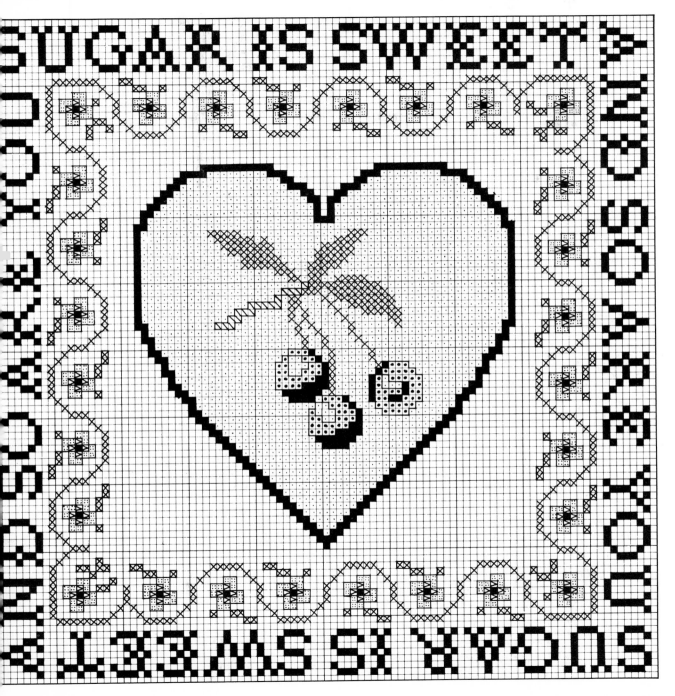

Roses are red,

Violets are blue,

Sugar is sweet

And so are you.

■ Red, 606
⊙ Dark Pink, 603
⊡ Light Pink, 776
⊠ Green, 905
⊞ Blue, 793
⊵ Dark Blue, 797
◨ Brown, 610
■ Flower centers, Yellow, 444

Suggested technique:
  cross-stitch, half-cross, or
  continental stitch
Suggested applications:
  pillow, framed wall piece,
  clothing, rug

There was a little man, and
he had a little gun,
And his bullets were made
of lead, lead, lead;
He went to the brook, and
shot a little duck,
Right through the middle of
the head, head, head.

◩ Green, 701
◩ Rust, 918
☐ Snow White
■ Black, 310
⊞ Gray, 414
⊠ Blue Green, 517
◪ Gold, 741
◩ Green, 913
◉ Dark Orange, 900
⊡ Skin tone, 676, 434, 754, 760
   or Ecru
Outline stitch in face, Black,
   310

Suggested technique:
   cross-stitch
Suggested applications:
   pillow, clothing

Cock-a-doodle-doo!
My dame has lost her shoe,
And master's lost his
    fiddling stick,
And doesn't know what to
    do.

■ Red, 666
▣ Rust, 918
▦ Gold, 741
▨ Brown, 435
◙ Green, 905
▷ Orange, 947
◪ Black, 310
⊟ Blue Green, 517
◥ Yellow, 444
◩ Light Blue, 799
Ⅲ Yellow Green, 907
■ Eye, Black, 310
Outline stitch in feet, Black,
    310

Suggested technique:
    cross-stitch
Suggested applications:
    pillow, clothing

Tom, Tom, the piper's son,
Stole a pig and away he
    run;
The pig was eat,
And Tom was beat,
And Tom went howling
    down the street.

⊞ Peach, 352
■ Light Blue, 799
◨ Rust, 918
⊠ Green, 905
◪ Gray Brown, 611
⊪ Light Peach, 353
◉ Dark Blue, 797
◙ Light Yellow, 743
⊗ Black, 310
⊡ Skin tone, 676, 434, 754, 760
    or Ecru
Outline stitch in pig, Black, 310
French knot for boy's nose,
    Rust, 918

Suggested technique:
    cross-stitch
Suggested applications:
    pillow, clothing

Old Mother Hubbard

Went to the cupboard,

To fetch her poor dog a

bone;

But when she got there

The cupboard was bare

And so the poor dog had

none.

⊠ Red Violet, 917
⊙ Dark Pink, 603
■ Black, 310
◪ Yellow, 444
⊞ Light Blue, 809
⊡ Skin tone, 676, 434, 754, 760
  or Ecru
◪ Tan, 976
⊡ Gray, 451
■ Mouth, Dark Pink, 603
☐ Snow White
Outline stitch in dog, hands,
  Black, 310

Suggested technique:
  cross-stitch
Suggested applications:
  framed wall piece, clothing

There was a fat man of
  Bombay,
Who was smoking one
  sunshiny day;
When a bird called a snipe
Flew away with his pipe,
Which vexed the fat man of
  Bombay.

⊠ Red Violet, 917
■ Red, 606
⊠ Gray, 415
⊙ Orange, 947
⊠ Dark Pink, 603
⊞ Green, 912
⊠ Blue Green, 518
⊙ Gold, 741
⊟ Green, 906
⊡ Flesh tone, 434
■ Eyes, Black, 310
☐ Eyes, Snow White
Outline stitch in face, Black,
  310
Optional for half-cross or
  continental stitch only:
  background, Snow White

Suggested technique:
  cross-stitch, half-cross, or
  continental stitch
Suggested applications:
  pillow, framed wall piece,
  quilt

Needlepoint Applications
Projects, Patterns, and Ideas

The following projects are designed for those who wish to combine their needlepoint expertise with other skills already familiar to them. If you like, you may alter the designs or color schemes to satisfy your imagination as well as your capabilities. Or, you may choose other patterns from the book and adapt them to the following projects. Why not personalize your project by adding your initials and the year to the design (see page 60 for alphabet and numbers pattern).

Keep in mind that these patterns needn't be applied to the given projects, but can simply be stitched and then mounted or framed. Whenever possible, we have included the exact amounts of wool or thread necessary to complete the pattern. If you are unable to estimate the amounts yourself, seek the help of your storekeeper.

The suggested applications offer a variety of needlepoint display—let them inspire you to do many more of your own.

Polly put the kettle on,
Polly put the kettle on,
Polly put the kettle on,
We'll all have tea.

■ Brown, 801
☒ Light Blue, 809
▣ Lavender, 553
▥ Pink, 3326
▢ Light Yellow, 743
▨ Light Green, 368

Suggested technique:
   cross-stitch
Suggested applications: tea
   cozy

Polly put the kettle on
A tea cozy

Grid Size: 131 x 101 squares
Stitch: cross-stitch
Materials: 10 squares-per-inch, beige Pearl Aida cloth, cut 13½ x 16½ inches; cotton embroidery floss: 2 skeins each of light green, pink, light yellow, violet; 3 skeins light blue; 4 to 5 skeins dark brown; #7 embroidery needle; ½ yard Aida cloth or cotton (45 inches wide) in a harmonizing color; 2 pieces of cotton or Dacron quilt filling, each 9½ x 12½ inches (plus a little extra for the sides); scissors; 1-inch-wide masking tape (optional); soft pencil; thread for basting; towel; wooden or composition board for blocking; Contact paper; rustproof tacks; straight pins; small ribbon or cloth loop (optional).
Procedure: Your fabric should be cut so that you have the required number of squares plus 2 inches on all sides. To prevent fraying, overcast* or tape the raw edges of your cloth. To form the pattern grid on your cloth, follow procedure outlined in Basic Project 1. You should now have a grid of 131 x 101 squares in the center of your cloth.

Begin pattern by cross-stitching the outer and inner dark brown borders. Next, outline the teapot in half-cross stitch. Then fill in the colored stripes on the pot before filling in the teapot body. Lastly, stitch in the colors within the border design. Remove the grid of basting threads from the fabric. Do not yet remove the tape or overcasting from the edges. Gently wash the fabric in lukewarm water and mild soapsuds. Rinse well and roll up in a towel to extract the excess water (do not wring or squeeze the fabric).

To block, stretch the fabric over a wooden or composition board that you have covered on one side with Contact paper (the Contact paper prevents the wood from staining your fabric). Tack down each corner with rustproof tacks. Pulling the fabric taut as you work, tack the middle of each side and at 2-inch intervals all around the edge. When the fabric is thoroughly dry, remove the tacks and the edge binding. Cut the excess border fabric down to 1 inch on all sides.

From the Aida cloth or the cotton in a harmonizing color, cut three pieces, each 11½ x 14½ inches (see Fig. 1). Allowing 1-inch seam allowances everywhere, and with right sides together, sew the teapot and one of the plain pieces together along only the top 14½-inch edge (see Fig. 2). To form the inner lining of the tea cozy, sew the remaining two pieces together along the top 14½-inch edge (see Fig. 3). Baste a piece of quilt filling to the wrong side of each of the plain sections of the inner lining (see Fig. 4). To make the ends of the tea cozy, cut four 5 x 12-inch pieces from the plain cloth, rounding the top edges as shown in Fig. 5. To join two of these ends to the inner tea cozy, run a basting thread through the curved edge of each end piece. With right sides together, position the end so that the center of the curve aligns with the top seam of the cozy. Then ease in the fullness along the top curve and stitch to the inner lining (see Fig. 6). Repeat the same procedure to join the ends to the outer tea cozy. Now place the outer and inner tea cozy together with right sides to the inside. Pin and then sew along one bottom side. Turn the cozy right side out, stuff a small amount of quilt filling into each end piece, and stitch the last edge together by hand. Quilt* or tuft* the tea cozy to hold the filling in place. If you wish to hang your tea cozy on the wall when not in use, simply stitch a small ribbon or cloth loop to one corner.

Fig. 1

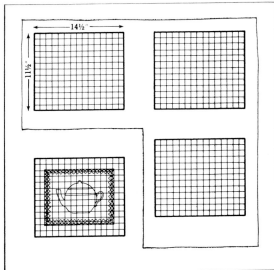

Fig. 2

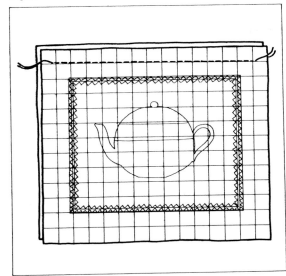

Fig. 3

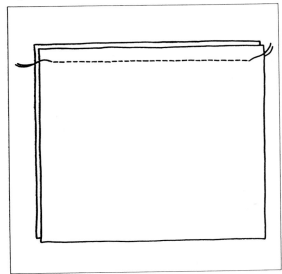

Fig. 4

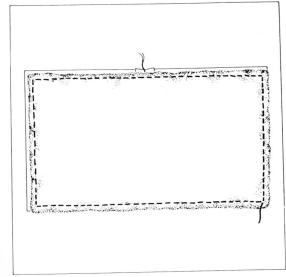

Fig. 5

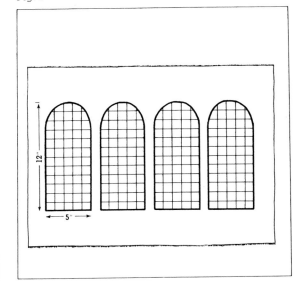

Fig. 6

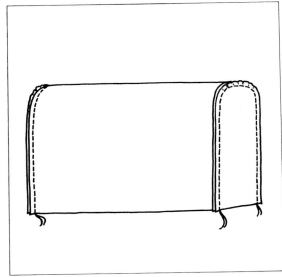

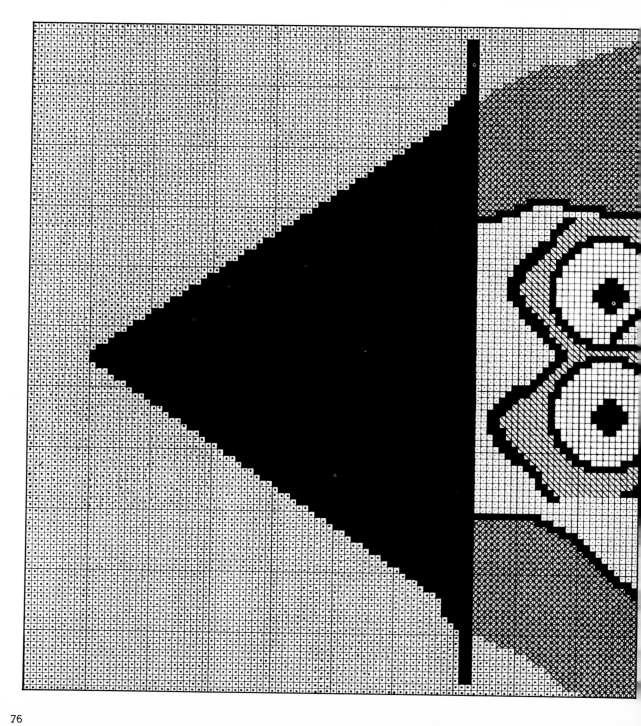

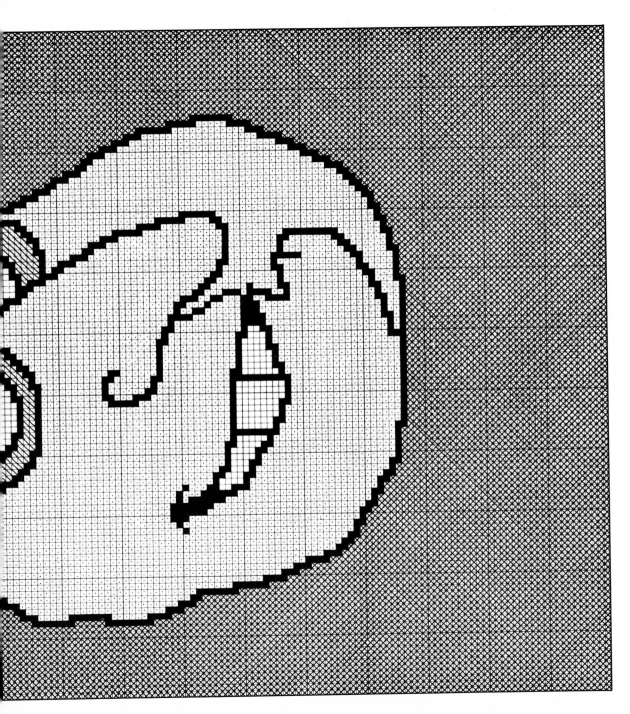

Hinx, minx, the old witch
    winks,
The fat begins to fry,
Nobody at home but
    Jumping Joan,
Father, Mother, and I.
Stick, stock, stone dead,
Blind men can't see;
Every knave will have a
    slave,
You or I must be he.

⊠ Gold, 972
■ Black, 310
☐ Snow White
⊡ Light Green, 369
⧄ Green, 701
⊙ Light Blue, 799

Suggested technique: basket-
    weave and continental stitch
Suggested applications: rug

Hinx minx
A needlepoint rug

Grid size: 110 x 200 squares
Stitch: basket-weave and continental
Materials: 4 squares-per-inch interlock canvas, cut 32 x 54 inches; colorfast Scheepjes Smyrna and Scheepjes Rya wool;[‡] #13 tapestry needle; masking tape; graph paper or photostat of pattern; colorfast marker; standing frame (optional); steam iron; pressing cloth; old door or wallboard; rustproof tacks; old sheet (optional); plastic bag (optional); scissors; carpet thread (optional); rug binding in blending color.
Procedure: Tape the edges of your canvas with masking tape. Using a colorfast marker, transfer the pattern onto the canvas by one of the methods given in Basic Project 2. As you transfer, remember that the basket-weave and the continental stitch are worked on a diagonal, across the intersection of the canvas threads. Therefore, be sure to transfer the pattern squares so that their centers correspond to two crossed threads on your canvas. Because this pattern is so simple, it is not necessary to color in the canvas.

The basket-weave stitch is the strongest stitch to use on a rug and it usually will not distort the canvas. However, begin by using the continental stitch to outline the different areas of color. (The continental stitch works around curves more easily, yet it resembles the basket-weave.) Then fill in each area using the basket-weave stitch. As you work, try to keep your stitches even to avoid distorting the canvas. Blocking the finished rug will straighten the shape somewhat, but a badly distorted rug will slowly revert back to its crooked shape. You should not have this trouble if you use the basket-weave stitch, but if you use the continental stitch for the entire rug, lash your rug to a standing frame. It is slower to work on a frame, but your finished rug will have a more even texture.

After you have completed stitching the rug, block it. There are several ways to block a rug, but there is just one principle to remember—you want to wet the wool and the sizing on the canvas, without washing the sizing away. If your rug is not badly distorted, merely steam-iron it using a damp pressing cloth, and let it dry for 12 hours. Another method is to stretch the rug taut on an old door or wallboard, and secure it with rustproof tacks, taking care not to drive the tacks through the canvas threads (see Fig. 1). Then steam-press the rug using a damp pressing cloth. A

third way to block your rug is to wet an old sheet and wring out the excess water. Roll up your rug in the sheet, wrap the roll in a plastic bag and let stand for 4 or 5 hours. Now tack the rug onto an old door or wallboard, pulling it into shape as you tack. Allow the rug to dry completely before removing it.

After your rug has dried, remove the edge tape and clip the canvas edges to 1 inch on every side. Using carpet thread or leftover rug wool, whipstitch* or overcast* rug binding to the top of the canvas, along the very edge of your stitching (see Fig. 2). Fold the binding tape under and whipstitch it down tightly to the underside of the rug (see Fig. 3).

[‡]We recommend using Scheepjes Rya wool for the blue, black, and dark green design areas. Although Smyrna wool is easier to handle, the Rya affords brighter shades. Four strands of Rya provide the same coverage as one strand of Smyrna.

Fig. 1

Fig. 2

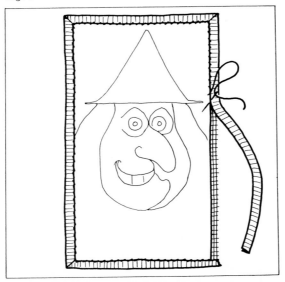

Fig. 3

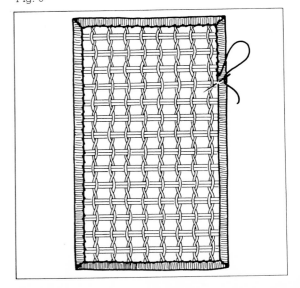

Hickory, dickory, dock,

The mouse ran up the

clock.

The clock struck one,

The mouse ran down,

Hickory, dickory, dock.

■ Black, 310
☒ Light Blue, 799
⊡ Tan, 976
☑ Gray, 647
Straight stitch for mice
    whiskers, Black, 310

Suggested technique:
    cross-stitch
Suggested applications: clock
    face

Hickory, dickory, dock
A clock face

Grid size: 84 x 84 squares
Stitch: cross-stitch
Materials: Aida or Pearl Aida cloth (same dimensions as clock face, plus 2 inches on each side); cotton embroidery floss; #7 embroidery needle; clock case and simple wind-up movement; scissors; masking tape; soft pencil; thread for basting; towel; wooden or composition board for blocking; contact paper; rustproof tacks; piece of cardboard or wood to fit inside clock case; staple gun and short staples; white glue.
Procedure: Figure the amount of cloth that you need to stitch this pattern according to the size of your clock face. This pattern was designed to fit an 8-inch-square clock face. You may enlarge or reduce the design to suit your needs. Cut your cloth large enough to accommodate the pattern (84 x 84 squares) plus an extra 2 inches on all sides for turn-under.

To prevent fraying, tape the raw edges of the cloth with masking tape. To form the pattern grid on your cloth, refer to procedure given in Basic Project 1. You should have a grid of 84 x 84 squares in the center of your cloth.

Begin by stitching in the border and the corner designs. Then stitch in the numbers, locating them by matching their position on the pattern grid with your cloth grid. Lastly, cross-stitch in the mice.

Now, carefully remove the basting threads, one by one. Wash the fabric in warm water and gentle soapsuds. Rinse well. To block, roll the cloth in a towel to extract the excess moisture (do not wring or squeeze). Using rustproof tacks, secure the corners and sides of the fabric to a board which you have covered on one side with Contact paper (to prevent the wood from staining the cloth). After it has dried, remove the cloth and strip the masking tape from the edges.

The finished work will wrap around a piece of cardboard or wood that you have cut exactly to fit inside the clock case. Use short staples to hold the cloth to wood, or white glue to fix it to cardboard. Carefully miter* the corners and dab a bit of white glue on the cloth edges to prevent raveling. For clock hands, cut out a tiny hole in the center of the face, and coat the clipped raw edges with white glue. Insert hands. Place the face in the case, secure it with glue or tacks if necessary, and wind up your clock!

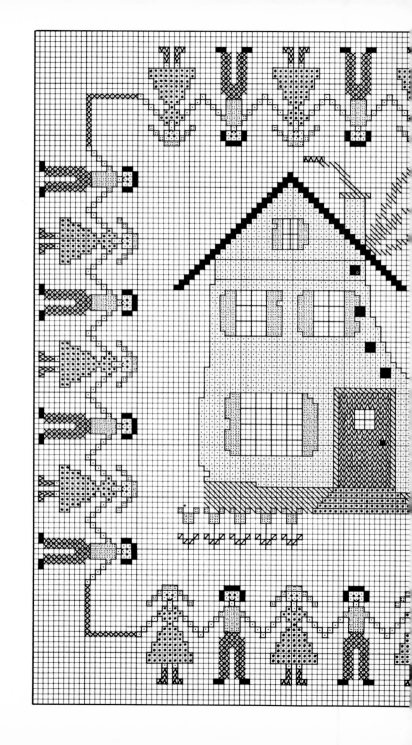

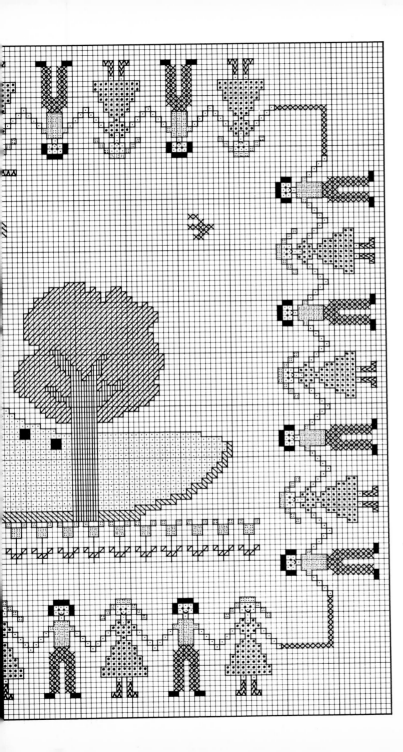

There was an old woman
who lived in a shoe,
She had so many children
she didn't know what to
do;
She gave them some broth
without any bread;
She whipped them all
soundly and put them to
bed.

⊠ Dark Blue, 797
⊡ Red, 666
⊞ Yellow, 444
⊿ Green, 905
■ Black, 310
◪ Gold, 741
⊡ Big Shoe, Light Brown, 436
◩ Rust, 918
⊞ Gray brown, 611
⊡ Skin tone for faces, 676, 434,
   754, 760 or Ecru
Outline stitch in big shoe,
   windows, steps, Black, 310
Outline stitch for mouths,
   Black, 310
French knot for eyes, Black,
   310

Suggested technique:
   cross-stitch
Suggested applications:
   clothing, pillow, framed
   wall piece, quilt

There was an old woman
A child's smock (size 6)

Grid size: 150 x 110 squares‡
Stitch: cross-stitch
Materials: 10 squares-per-inch, white Pearl Aida cloth (1½ yards, at least 26 inches wide); cotton embroidery floss: 4 skeins light brown; 2 skeins each of bright blue, bright red, bright green, bright yellow, orange, rust; 1 skein each of gray brown, black, skin tone or ecru; #7 embroidery needle; scissors; soft pencil; thread for basting; masking tape; brown paper; straight pins; sewing machine; iron; white cotton batiste for smock lining (1½ yards, at least 26 inches wide); 8 ½-inch-wide, flat white buttons (red dress is made of 100% cotton and adapted from Simplicity #7199, size 6, with puffed sleeves and added round collar).
Procedure: This project should be attempted only by an experienced seamstress. From Pearl Aida cloth, cut a piece large enough to accommodate pattern (150 x 110 squares) and allow an extra 4½ inches at the top, 6 inches on each side, and 2½ inches at the bottom (see Fig. 1). Use masking tape to bind the edges of your cloth. Make a pattern grid on the cloth according to the procedure outlined in Basic Project 1. Proceed to cross-stitch the pattern, noting that the top row of design figures has been eliminated to fit the smock front.

‡Grid size eliminates top row of pattern figures to fit smock. If you wish to stitch entire pattern, change figures accordingly.

When stitching is completed, remove the masking tape from the edges. To make the smock pattern, draw a grid of lines, spaced 1 inch apart, on brown paper. Using the grid as a guide, scale up the front, front yoke, and back of the smock as shown in Fig. 2. Cut out the pattern pieces. Center the front pattern piece over the cross-stitched Aida cloth, carefully noting the position of the cross-stitched design. Lay the front yoke and back pattern pieces on the plain Aida cloth (see Fig. 3). Pin and cut around the pattern pieces. Using the same three patterns, cut out the white cotton batiste lining. Machine-stitch the Aida cloth front to the front yoke, and the front lining to the yoke lining. Press the seams open. With right sides together, stitch the Aida cloth front and the lining front together, leaving a small opening along the side edge for turning (see Fig. 4). Clip the corners, turn right side out, and press. With right sides together, stitch the Aida cloth back and lining back together, again leaving an opening along the edge for turning (see Fig. 4). Clip corners, turn, and press. Stitch the side openings by hand. Make buttonholes on the shoulders and side tabs as shown in Fig. 5, and sew the buttons in place.

Fig. 1

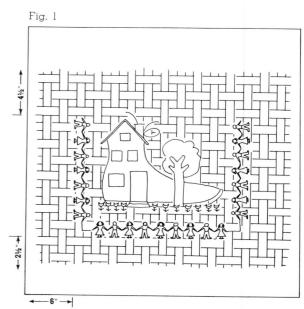

4½"

2½"

6"

Fig. 2

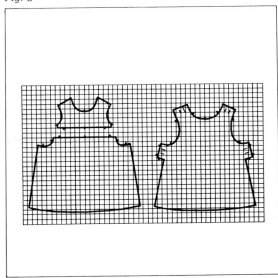

Fig. 3

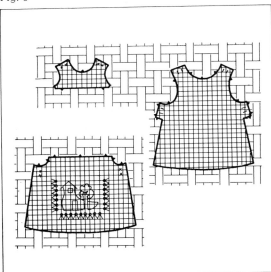

Fig. 4

Fig. 5

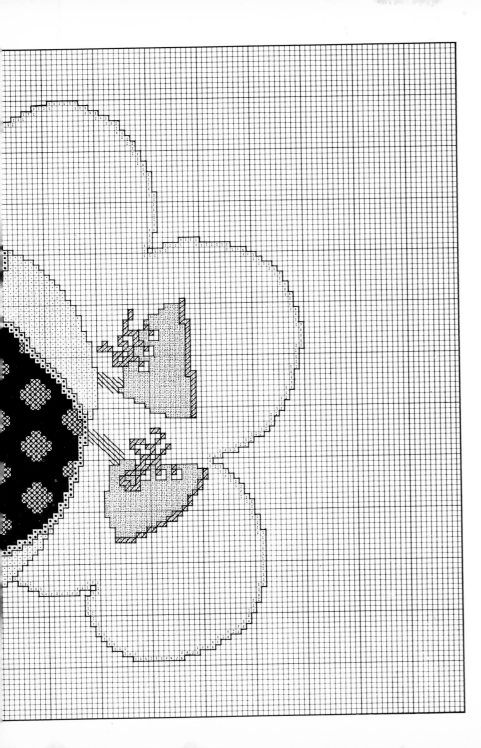

Goosey, goosey, gander,

Where shall I wander?

⊞ Green, 905
☒ Dark Pink, 603
◪ Red, 606
▨ Orange, 947
⊡ Yellow, 444
■ Blue Green, 813
◉ Purple, 209
⊡ Light Gray, 415
☐ Snow White
◩ Gray, 318
⊡ Light Blue, 799
■ Eye, Black, 310
Outline stitch in eye, shoe
  eyelets, Black, 310

Suggested technique:
  cross-stitch
Suggested applications: quilt,
  pillow, clothing

Old Mother Goose,
She had a son Jack,
A plain-looking lad
He was not very good
Nor yet very bad.

- ⊡ Light Gray, 415
- ⊞ Light Blue, 799
- ☑ Orange, 947
- ◪ Green, 905
- ⠿ Red, 606
- ■ Yellow, 444
- ⊙ Purple, 209
- ■ Eye, Black, 310

Outline stitch in eye, Black, 310

Suggested technique:
    cross-stitch
Suggested applications: quilt,
    pillow, clothing

Mother Goose Family
A quilt

Grid size: 136 x 109 squares (Goosey Gander); 65 x 75 squares (Son Jack)
Stitch: cross-stitch
Materials: 7½ yards medium-blue cotton (45 inches wide) for quilt top and bottom; 2½ yards lightweight white cotton; 1 bag Dacron pillow stuffing; 1 inexpensive, lightweight double-bed blanket; ½ yard scrim (10 squares per inch); cotton embroidery floss or Persian wool; #7 embroidery needle; scissors; graph paper or photostat of pattern; tracing paper; straight pins; soft pencil; sewing machine.
Procedure: Attempt this project only if you are an experienced sewer. From the blue cotton, cut forty-four 10 x 10-inch squares and one 19 x 19-inch square (see Fig. 1). Redraw the outlines of the goose figures and clouds for all three patterns on pages 86-89 on ten-squares-to-the-inch graph paper or enlarge, using a photostat as described in Project 2. Trace both cloud shapes, including one horizontal and one vertical line from the grid to align with the grain of your fabric. Draw an extra ¼-inch seam allowance all around the clouds for turn-under (see Fig. 2). From the white cotton, trace and then cut out 44 small clouds and 1 large cloud (pages 86–87), making sure that the direction of the fabric grain corresponds to the pattern grid on the tracing. To turn under seam allowance, clip the edges of each cloud ¼ inch all the way around. Pin

down this hem, if you wish, and then press or baste the seam allowance (see Fig. 3). Before stitching, make sure the fabric grain of the clouds is aligned with the fabric grain of the squares. Proceed to machine-stitch 42 of the clouds to the center of the squares, inserting Dacron pillow stuffing in each cloud before you complete the stitching.

Baste the remaining two small clouds and one large cloud to their respective squares. Cut one piece of scrim 10 x 15 inches and two pieces of scrim, each 6 x 7 inches. Lay the scrim over each basted cloud, aligning the mesh of the scrim with the weave of the clouds. Baste the scrim in place by stitching along each edge and diagonally across the piece (see Fig. 4). To help you begin the cross-stitch design, carefully note the position of the goose feet on each cloud pattern. Stitch all three figures from the feet up, following the pattern squares. Working over the scrim, make sure that each stitch goes through the fabric underneath. Do not catch the scrim with your thread. When you have completed stitching, dampen the scrim with water and carefully pull the individual threads of the scrim from under the stitching (remove the horizontal threads before the vertical threads). Now machine-stitch each cloud in place, inserting stuffing around the cross-stitching before you complete sewing all around the cloud (see Fig. 5).

Refer to Fig. 6 to position and sew all the quilt squares together, allowing ½-inch seam allowances. First make rows of squares, and then machine-stitch the rows together. Lay the quilt top over your blanket, and baste across the middle in both directions and around the edges. Trim off any excess blanket. To make the quilt bottom, piece the blue cotton together to same size as top. Pin it to the quilt top. Again, baste across the middle in both directions and around edges. Quilt* or tuft* the corners of each square. Machine-stitch 3-inch-wide bias strips of blue cotton around the edges on the right side of quilt. Miter* corners. Fold bias strips to back side of quilt, turn raw edges under and hand-stitch to back side.

Fig. 1

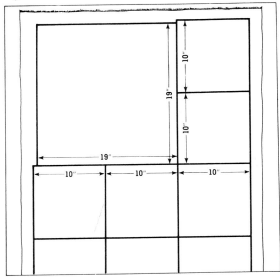

Fig. 2

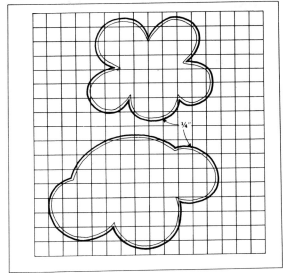

Fig. 3

Fig. 4

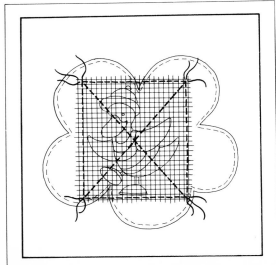

Fig. 5

Fig. 6

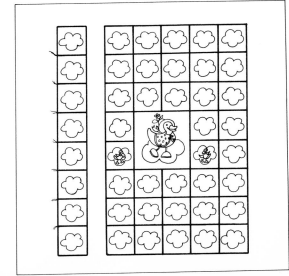

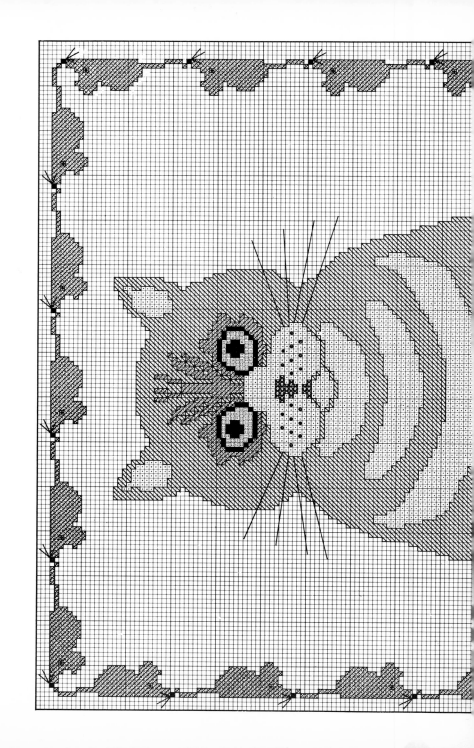

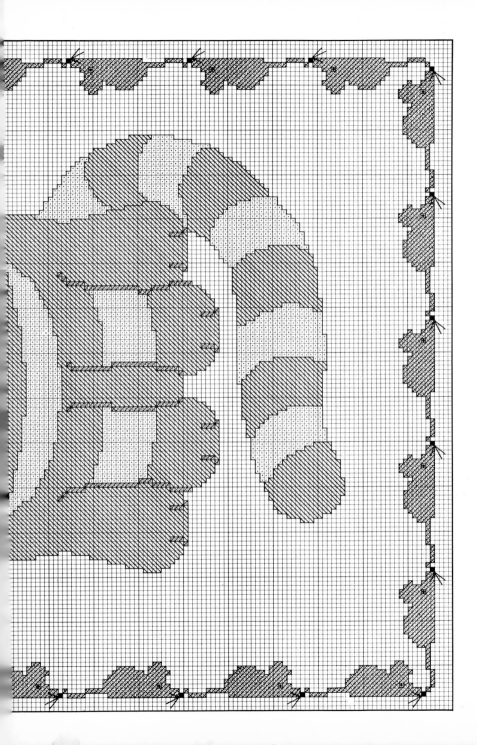

Pussy cat, pussy cat,
Where have you been?
I've been to London
To look at the Queen.
Pussy cat, pussy cat,
What did you there?
I frightened a little mouse
Under her chair.

☑ Gold, 740
⊡ Snow White
⊠ Pink, 604
⊞ Green, 471
■ Dark Brown, 902
⊠ Brown, 781
◉ Dark Blue, 797
Straight stitch for cat's
    whiskers, Snow White,
    or Dark Brown, 902
Straight stitch for mice
    whiskers, Dark Brown, 902
French knots for spots on cat's
    nose, Brown, 781

Suggested technique:
    continental, basket-weave,
    or cross-stitch
Suggested applications:
    stuffed toy, framed wall
    piece, rug

Pussy cat, pussy cat

A stuffed toy

Grid Size: 120 x 170 squares[‡]
Stitch: continental or basket-weave
Materials: 10-squares-per-inch interlock canvas, cut 14 x 19 inches; colorfast Persian wool; #8 tapestry needle; cloth backing (corduroy, wool, or flannel), 14 x 19 inches; cotton or Dacron pillow stuffing; scissors; 1-inch-wide masking tape (optional); graph paper or photostat of pattern; colorfast marker; crayons (optional); sewing machine; straight pins; thread, in color to match backing.
Procedure: Take liberties with this pattern and turn the central cat into a stuffed toy by eliminating the mouse border design.

Bind the raw edges of your canvas with masking tape or with an overcast stitch*. Transfer the cat pattern to canvas according to one of the methods given in Basic Project 2. As you transfer the pattern, remember that the basket-weave and the continental stitch differ from the cross-stitch in that they do not form a square over the canvas holes; instead, they make a diagonal across the intersection of the canvas threads. Therefore, you must transfer the pattern squares so that their centers correspond to two crossed threads on the canvas. If you wish, you may color the design areas on the canvas.

[‡] Grid size is for cat figure only; if you wish to stitch entire pattern (including mouse border) for framing, change figures accordingly.

Stitch in the pattern using either the continental or basket-weave stitch. (The basket-weave was used for the stuffed cat shown in Plate 6.) When you have finished, overcast* or whipstitch* around the entire outside edge of the cat, skipping one hole between each stitch (see Fig. 1). If possible, also run a machine zig-zag or straight stitch* around the outside of the overcasting just to make sure that the canvas threads will hold in place when you cut out the cat. You will have to improvise when you overcast between the tail and the feet, as the space is tight. Now cut out the cat; then cut your backing to the same size and shape as your cutout. Machine-stitch the edges of the backing as you did with the cat. Carefully pin the two pieces together, right sides facing, and then machine-stitch around the edges, leaving a 4-inch opening on one side of the cat's body and a 2 to 3-inch opening on the bottom side of the tail (see Fig. 2). Turn cat right side out. Insert stuffing through openings and stitch closed by hand with matching thread (see Fig. 3).

Fig. 1

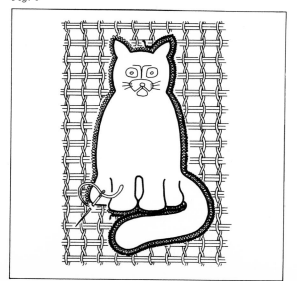

Fig. 2

Glossary

even weave: a fabric weave in which the number of warp threads exactly equals the number of weft threads for every measured inch of fabric.

irregular weave: a fabric weave in which the warp threads do not exactly equal the weft threads per measured inch of fabric; or, a fabric in which either warp or weft threads are completely covered one by the other.

latch hooking: a technique used for knotting a pile rug in which each knot is made from a measured length of precut rug wool that is pulled through an open square of double-threaded canvas with a special tool called a latch hook.

mesh: the holes formed between the vertical and horizontal threads of canvas.

miter: a tuck made in a corner, taking up the excess fabric and pulling it tightly so that the corner is square and even.

overcast stitch (whipstitch): to sew with evenly spaced slanting stitches over the edge of a fabric.

petit point: needlepoint done on canvas that is 20 meshes to the inch or finer.

ply: a single strand of yarn. One or more strands may be twisted together to form plied yarn.

quilt: joining together two pieces of fabric and filling with tiny running stitches.

selvage: finished edge of the fabric as it is rolled off the bolt; the edge formed by the weft thread as it turns to re-cross the warp.

straight stitch (running): the most basic sewing stitch; the needle runs in and out of the fabric.

tuft: joining together two pieces of fabric and filling by passing a strong thread through them and tying it in a knot, usually on the back side.

warp: vertical threads that run in the same direction as the selvage of the fabric. These are the threads that are held in tension on a loom.

weft: horizontal threads that run perpendicular to the selvage of the fabric.

worsted: yarn made from long wool fibers that are combed and laid parallel before spinning. Plied worsted yarn has a distinctive-looking twist.

Fig. 3

Suppliers

In all my journeys to needlework stores, I have never found one that can compare to Albert and Ilse Wiener's stores in Sausalito, California. The Handcraft From Europe stores are not only a delight to see, they also always have a wide range of the best quality materials, friendly service, and patience to help with whatever problems you might have. Don't hesitate to write them if you are having difficulty in locating any materials.

The following stores carry most of the materials mentioned in this book:

U.S.A. East

Papillon
375 Pharr Road
Northeast Atlanta, Georgia 30305

Earth Guild/Grateful Union
Department N
15 North Tudor Street
Cambridge, Massachusetts 02139

Nantucket Needleworks
Nantucket Island, Massachusetts 02554

The Stitchery
204 Worcester Turnpike
Wellesley Hills, Massachusetts 02181

Boutique Margot
26 West 54th Street
New York, New York 10019

Selma's Art Needlework
1645 Second Avenue
New York, New York 10028

Bon Bazar, Ltd.
149 Waverly Place
New York, New York 10014

Coulter Studios, Inc.
118 East 59th Street
New York, New York 10022

Alice Maynard
724 Fifth Avenue
New York, New York 10019

Needle's Point
1626 Macon
McLean, Virginia 24503

U.S.A. Middlewest

The Swedish Style Knitting Shop
5209 North Clark Street
Chicago, Illinois 60640

Needle Nest
729 East Lake Street
Wayzata, Minnesota 55391

Scandinavian Art Handicraft
7696 Camargo Road, Maderira
Cincinnati, Ohio 45243

Maribee
Department B-77
2904 West Lancaster
Fort Worth, Texas 76107

Needle Art Studio
17700 Capitol Drive
Brookfield, Wisconsin 53005

U.S.A. West

Laraway's
313 Marine Avenue
Balboa Island, California 92662

Warp, Woof and Potpourri
514 North Lake Avenue
Pasadena, California 91101

Jed's Needlecrafts
3959 State Street
Santa Barbara, California 93105

Handcraft From Europe
P.O. Box 372
Store: 1201 Bridgeway Boulevard
Sausalito, California 94965

Thumbelina Needlework
1685 Copenhagen
Solvang, California 93463

The Handweaver
460 First Street, East
Sonoma, California 95476

Arachne Webworks
2309 N.W. Thurman
Portland, Oregon 97210

Phalice's Thread Web
West 1301 14th Avenue
Spokane, Washington 99204

Rug Supplies

Yarn 'n Rug Works
95 North Raymond Avenue
Pasadena, California 91103

William Condon & Sons
65 Queen Street
Charlottetown, Prince Edward Island
Canada

Carlbert Rug Supplies
P.O. Box 84
Portland, Maine 04112